DON'T MISS

THE *P*OINT

RAY BEESON

Overcomers Ministries
Ventura, California

Overcomers Ministries
7357 Wolverine St.
Ventura, CA 93003
www.overcomersministries.net

Library of Congress Cataloging in Publication Data

Don't Miss The Point
Copyright @ 2007 by Ray Beeson

Published by Overcomers Ministries
Ventura, CA

ISBN 0-9748269-2-8

Unless otherwise noted, Scripture references are from the
New King James Version of the Bible, Thomas Nelson, Inc., Publishers.

"Ointment and perfume delight the heart, /And the sweetness of a man's friend *gives delight* by hearty counsel" (Pro 27:9).

To Friends:
Andy, Don, Steve

Thanks to Darrel Faxon and Rick Kline for their valuable contributions in walking through the manuscript with me. Also, thanks to Tom and Gayle McCauley for their very special help as well.

Other Books by Ray Beeson:

The Real Battle
That I May Know Him
Spiritual Warfare and Your Children—co-written
Strategic Spiritual Warfare—co-written
The Hidden Price of Greatness—co-written
Create In Me A Clean Heart
In Memory of Joseph Greycloud

"For in Him we live and move and have our being" (Acts 17:28).

Contents:

Portions of some Scriptures have been highlighted by the use of **Bold Print**. This is added for emphasis.

To Begin:

In the overall structure and content of the Bible there is a single thread uniquely woven into the text—God's desire to reconcile people to Himself. There is also a single predominate human need—His presence.

According to the book of Genesis, all human suffering and sorrow rests solely on the absence of God's Spirit and a lack of the manifestation of His glory. This Bible account of human beginning and eventual pain might be considered a fable[1] if it were not so accurate in the description of, and the prescription for, human anguish. Even if it were simply a tale, it sets the stage for the unfolding of the rest of the Scriptures. Everything in the Bible is consistent with this description.

Genesis 3:6-7 describes the breaking of a relationship that initiated the problems humanity faces today. Adam and Eve broke covenant with God in such a way that He was forced to withdraw from them.

For as short as the story is in these few verses, it is quite possible that if the events were told in detail, it would take warehouses to contain the books. This was no small occurrence with no small outcome. The loss was immeasurable. The reason the story is not more fully explored in Scripture rests solely in God's hands. All He seems to want us to know is that something went wrong and with devastating consequences; and that from that point on He has been working to fix the problem.[2] By walking slowly and carefully through the following verses in Genesis 3 we get a picture of yesterday's events in a language still understandable today. Examining the details of this early relationship helps to understand a bit more of why our world exists as it does.

Introduction

In verse 8, upon hearing "the sound of the Lord God walking in the garden in the cool of the day, Adam and his wife tried to hide from God's presence among the trees of the garden." Something so traumatic had just taken place that they were unable to stand before Him. The thought of His presence caused such apprehension they could think of nothing but hiding themselves. The result was an increasing sense of distance between them and their Creator.

For as much as God tried to assure Adam (humanity) that He still wanted the relationship with its corresponding fellowship, Adam's faith to believe just wasn't there. Over and over again, throughout the Scriptures, God's message of reconciliation and restoration resounds. But the damage caused by sin to Adam's spirit and ours was extensive, and accepting God's word as true was overwhelming. Literally, it would take God stepping out of heaven[3] and into human form to make the way of reunion possible.[4] In verse 15 we get a foretaste of this remarkable advent in the form of Jesus. Here He is called the "Seed." From the very beginning God had in mind to bring mankind back to Himself by way of His Son.

In verse 9, God calls out, "Where are you?" Or, in other words, "Adam, what's going on?" This incredible relationship was initially tied together by way of agreement and shared responsibility, and Adam had violated the accord. The outcome is evident everywhere we look. But within the next verse we see the consequences of a broken covenant begin to unfold. Adam responds, "I heard Your voice in the garden, and *I was afraid* because I was naked." Not only is Adam now centered upon himself, as is evident by the number of times he uses the word "I" in this verse, but he has acquired the foreign element of fear. Not an ounce of emotional disturbance was found in God's presence prior to Adam's disgrace—no worry, anxiety, depression, or discouragement. Each day Adam and Eve walked in complete peace. Perfect love (God's presence) eliminated the potential for fear, as does His presence today in "casting" out fear (1 John 4:18). Adam recognized that the terror in his mind was the direct result of his nakedness. Physical nakedness was by no means the main issue. The loss of God's glory created spiritual nakedness. Previously, God's presence surrounded Adam and his wife in such a way that they lived clothed in His glory. We catch a glimpse of this in Satan's original name, Lucifer, which means "Light Bearer" or "Shining One," and in Moses, whose face shone as a result of God's presence on the mountain. Both experienced a brilliant change in their appearance as they stood before God.

God wants humanity to be re-clothed in His glory through Jesus. "But put on the Lord Jesus Christ, and make no provision for the flesh, to *fulfill its* lusts" (Rom 13:14). "For as many of you as were baptized into Christ have put on Christ" (Gal 3:27). "I will greatly rejoice in the LORD, /My soul shall be joyful in my God; For He has clothed me with the garments of salvation, /He has covered me with the robe of righteousness, /As a bridegroom decks *himself* with ornaments, /And as a bride adorns *herself* with her jewels" (Isa 61:10).

No matter how we talk about spiritual things in terms of words such as redemption, salvation, reconciliation, or sanctification, it all comes down to the simple fact—God wants humanity back into His presence. He wants to restore His glory, not just in eternity, but here and now. Make no mistake; this is foremost on God's mind. Not only were we *meant* for His glory, we can't survive without it.

The intent of the chapters that follow is to show that we cannot live satisfactorily in any kind of peaceful contentment without God's presence. Christianity was never meant to foster a way of life as much as it was designed to reestablish God's glory. Nothing is more important to God than a personal relationship with His creation, a connection established through Jesus and nurtured by His indwelling Spirit. Salvation is about Christ in us, the hope of glory.

---

1. Human knowledge, understanding, and reasoning do little to affirm the Scriptures. It is revelation by the Holy Spirit that causes us to believe the Bible. We know in our hearts and not so much in our minds that we can trust this amazing Book.

2. The intent here is not to suggest that God's sovereignty was minimized or that He in some way lost control of what He had created as if it were snatched from His hands.

3. "Let this mind be in you which was also in Christ Jesus, who, being in the form of God, did not consider it robbery to be equal with God, but made Himself of no reputation, taking the form of a bondservant, *and* coming in the likeness of men. And being found in appearance as a man, He humbled Himself and became obedient to *the point of* death, even the death of the cross" (Phil 2:5-8).

4. The Israelite people living prior to the coming of Jesus were saved through covenant relationship with God. In that particular relationship they were taught the necessity of blood as a payment for sin. Animal blood became the payment until the true Payment (Substitute) came.

Chapter 1:

Relationship Before Obligation

Segments of Christian thinking often emphasize righteousness as a way to establish a relationship with God. The harsh legalisms of some churches are the outgrowth of an approach that stresses personal performance as the only way to please God. A careful examination of Scripture reveals something quite different. The Bible teaches that it is a relationship with God that establishes righteousness. This is evident from relationships God has had with people in the past, one of the first found in the Old Testament, "Abraham believed God, and it was accounted to him for righteousness" (Rom 4:3).

Should there be the slightest tinge of desire for spiritual things relating to God, one generally finds an array of issues and obstacles that stand in the way. Questions concerning His character, and especially reservations and uncertainties relating specifically to His goodness scatter the road to understanding who He is and how to relate to Him. They usually begin with the word "why?" and travel through a collection of age-old questions about the sufferings and sorrows of our world in light of biblical references to His goodness, kindness, and mercy.

Then there is the matter of attire. What kind of spiritual garment is necessary in order to come before the God Who is arrayed in splendor and clothed in glory? In other words, what is the spiritual dress code? Is our apparel appropriate? No matter how we approach the subject, it always leads to the need for a clarification and intensification of righteousness in order to enter His presence. But if righteousness is approached incorrectly, life becomes a struggle between right and wrong, as well as track and field events filled with jumps, hurdles, and races.

When the issue is righteousness inquiries abound, beginning with what it is and how we are to obtain it. These are two of the major questions in life and have always deeply affected both society and religion. There are no shortages of commentaries on the topics of how to live together properly as people or of how to please a holy and righteous God.

Nearly fifty years ago, Leonard Ravenhill in his notable book, "Why Revival Tarries" denounced the Church for its failure to keep the standards of the Scriptures. Prior to him Dietrich Bonhoeffer claimed that numerous Christians had opted for "cheap grace," a statement decrying the deficient way many conduct their lives while they simultaneously argue that God's grace is sufficient for their delinquent behavior.

Often we, too, are disturbed by the way some churches function and by the manner in which many Christians structure their lives, especially when it comes to right living. There is nothing new concerning difficulties relating to Christianity and to the people who claim to be its followers. And holiness and righteousness are often at the heart of the issue.

For all the analysis that is readily forthcoming: lack of commitment, carnality, apathy, lethargy, selfish interests, and the cares of this life, there is one reason for the struggles facing the Christian church, especially in America, that we might want to consider in more detail. It has to do directly with Jesus Himself.

If Christianity is ever said to have failed, a debatable subject, I'd like to suggest that the failure rests mostly on a lessened emphasis of the person of Jesus, and especially on a lack of understanding of the reality and potential of His indwelling Spirit. A major part of the gospel is the message that the Holy Spirit has come, not only to walk with a person, but to live within him or her as well (John 14:17). The implication is that without Jesus (His Spirit literally living in the human frame, although Jesus, Himself, is seated at the right hand of the Father) we have no ability to perform the righteousness necessary both to please God and to assure a safe and sane world. Yet, much of the Christian community, when speaking of Jesus, mentions Him as having gone away to heaven to return some day in the future, but not uniquely present in Spirit now. Periodically, considerable emphasis is placed on the Holy Spirit, but much of it has to do with God's power displayed in miracles, or in the exhilaration brought about by the manifestation of His presence in worship services. And although there may be nothing wrong with these demonstrations, there is still little emphasis placed on character development and holy living created as a direct result of His presence and help. What strength do we have for holiness and righteousness if we do not draw it directly from God Himself? What future do we have for life if we are not somehow joined directly to heaven, the place of our citizenship (Phil 3:20)? And what hope do we have of celebrating a holy God if we ourselves are not entering into His likeness.

There is still another problem sometimes initiated by some within the Christian community. It is the assertion that intimacy with God is erroneous, that we cannot know Him personally. This error destroys the intent of the gospel, which is the working of Christ within a person "both to will and to do of His good pleasure" (Phil 2:13).

When the gospel is adapted to the culture, which it often is in the promotion of what God can do *for* people, rather than a means to *change* the culture, there remains little effort to define Christianity as a personal experience with God. If God is seen at all to be personal it is only for what He gives, and not for a walk with Him to change our lives. God's ways, then, are seen as plans to enhance life, as well as programs to make life easier.

Listen sometime to people talk about God and it is often in terms of what He has given them, how He has blessed them with things. I like the person who admits, "I was a selfish, egotistical, angry, person until God began to work in me. Now I'm changing."

Every road leading away from the God who came to live within, as well as the God whose presence marshals the accomplishment of His "will and good pleasure," has to do with detours, many of them emphasizing personal righteousness aside from His help, or ways and means to accomplishing good behavior by way of a set of rules. But no amount of self-imposed legalisms or self-help steps to a better life has ever brought about God's desire for intimacy with His people. None of these things have ever produced the life changes that take place in a moment when Jesus communicates within the human spirit. The point is simply that mankind's only hope is the "indwelling" Christ. The Christian life won't work and true righteousness will never be obtained without a personal and intimate experience with Jesus.

Some who preach and promote Christianity mistakenly emphasize performance over relationship. Knowledge of this error is nothing new. The recognition has been around for a

16

long time and has its roots in a rhetoric that says, "Rules without relationship end in rebellion." We may say we believe that righteousness flows out of relationship with God, but practice something quite different. In a survey, a group of Christians were asked to define Christianity. The answers weren't surprising. Most of them can be summed up from a single response: "Christianity: The act of following Christ and His teachings—a lifestyle." That is precisely what Christianity is not. It is neither an act nor a lifestyle. There are millions of people whose actions and lifestyles are indistinguishable from the best of Christians, and yet not one of them claims Christianity. You will wear out fast by trying to live the Christian life, unless you are constantly drawing your strength from Jesus.

What, then, is Christianity? It is Jesus living in a person by His Spirit. In that way, Christianity is not a lifestyle, but rather a life. It is the very life of Christ resident in the inner recesses of the human spirit, and there only because He has been invited to enter. Poor is the person who believes that his or her first obligation to their faith is to live a particular way of life. But, often this they are taught in a language that warns, "You'll never please God unless you start doing better."

If personal righteousness were a means for pleasing God, then pride, already the deadliest of our enemies, would know no limits. The sin that plunged Lucifer from the courts of glory to the caverns of his own self-love easily corrodes the person whose faith is in his own abilities.

Even among the most dedicated of believers, those who long to hear the words "well done," there is the tendency to ratchet up personal performance to please the Master. Lest there be some misunderstanding, the intent here is not to suggest some kind of spiritual passivity to be practiced by

17

way of grace. The question is not whether or not we are to put forth effort, the question is, "by whose strength do we overcome?" The very words of Jesus make plain that without Him "we can do nothing." Had He said, "Without Me you can do but a little," or "Without Me your strength is limited," we would have had cause to use all of our talents and abilities to produce a righteous life. But His words were, "You can do nothing." In other words, add up all your self-effort, all your personal striving, and all your good deeds and the bottom line is still zero.

"Why, then, even try?" That's a good question. Expanded, the question really means, "Why should *I* try?" And, again it is easy to see that we can't seem to get away from the mentality that for God to accept us, we've got to get our lives into a program that pleases Him. In other words, it's all about me and my ability to perform. This is why there are countless exhausted Christians everywhere suffering from guilt and condemnation. And in their exhaustion, they often do foolish things, not the least of which is to give up and go back into the world.

There is no question as to the need for righteousness, and that defined by the Scriptures. Good deeds are not an option. Again, the issue is where goodness originates. If it comes from personal effort or is defined by human wisdom and knowledge, it profits nothing. God must be present in the human spirit, illuminating His word and giving divine strength and understanding, or the outcome is nothing more or less than self-righteousness. This knowledge caused Paul to joyously proclaim, "I can do all things through Christ who strengthens me" (Phil 4:13).

How, then, is true righteousness to be manifested in a believer? The Apostle, Paul, and his Jewish brothers knew well that God demanded right living. A righteous and Holy

18

God would commune only with those who were willing to live within the integrity of His nature as defined by the Law. Paul thought he had done quite well in living up to the Old Testament Scriptures, at least until his encounter with Christ. From that point on, it wasn't only performance that mattered. Now attitude, motive, behavior, and the very spirit in which he did things became issues. This man with a former passionate self-styled religious life of hard personal work discovered that with all his effort to live a righteous life, he still had fallen light years short of the goal. The intensity of his agony is revealed in his statement, "O, wretched man that I am" (Rom 7:24). In a single moment the tattered and torn garment of his own righteousness was ripped from his weak and impoverished spirit. All he had worked so hard to accomplish vanished before his eyes. Had it not been for the splendor of a new hope in Jesus, Paul would have despaired with the pain that screams, "Woe *is* me, for I am undone!" (Isa 6:5).

No one likes to be told he or she is wrong; and worse yet, no one wants to find that years of hard work have been in vain. But Paul's self-built house of good deeds was gone and there was not a scrap of material with which to rebuild. Not Paul, not you, not me, literally no one is capable of sustaining that kind of disappointment without some feeling of devastation; not unless, like Paul, we have seen God's glory and purpose in Jesus and realize that all that stands in the way of a new life in Him is ourselves.

In Paul's pre-Christian analysis of his own abilities, and to some extent his trouble with the flesh after salvation, he acknowledged that the things he recognized as right behavior, he was completely incapable of doing. At the same time, he was forced to own up to doing things he knew were wrong (Rom 7:14-26). Paul wanted to do right, but simply couldn't. He even wanted to do God's will. His problem was living in a body that wanted no restraints. His dilemma was so strong it could be described as a violent inner storm from which he pleaded to be set free. "Who shall deliver me?" he wrote in expressing his pain. After bringing his readers to understand what he had been through, he then turns and focuses on Jesus, of whom Paul never ceases to speak. This great Apostle wanted nothing more in life than to know Jesus (Phil 3:10). Now it would be the life of Jesus personally manifested in him that would give him the ability to live right. His message, again and again, was about Jesus and Jesus' desire to live by His Spirit within the human spirit (Col 1:27).

Chapter 2:

Partakers of the Divine Nature

The gospel, far above living a holy and righteous life, is a message of partaking of the Divine Nature in Jesus. It is an expression of God's desire to work deep within the human spirit for reconciliation and restoration.

Ask a child where God is and the answer most likely will be, "in heaven." Ask how far away heaven is, and you will probably get, "A long way." That is not a concept reserved for children alone; it exists in adults as well, only with implications unknown to most children. The assumption is that not only is heaven distant, but so is God. That is sometimes why a great deal of prayer is offered up in order to get God to come down for a visit. Long prayers and fastings are frequently presented to overcome a reluctant God—to close the distance. The same mentality goes on to suggest that God is somewhat aloof when it comes to human affairs, making rare visits to check up on how well we are doing, and especially to see if we are doing what He has told us to do. This perceived remoteness gives rise to the sense that it is really up to us to forge through life doing the best we can. Then, when our best exhausts itself far short of the goal line, we need someone to blame, and often God and people are accused. If God and others manage to escape the accusation, then we blame ourselves while living deeply impacted by guilt and condemnation. And there is almost always someone around to confirm our self-indictment with a further paralyzing charge, "It looks like you are just going to have to try a little harder." That this is human religion is hardly debatable in view of its devastating consequences. How discouraging it is for others to harp on our failures, which we are well aware of. But sadly, it is what is often thought to be the core of Christianity, with some leaders firm in their belief that God has called them to tell people how to live right. How far that is from the call to tell people about the Jesus who can help them live properly, the Jesus Who, by His Spirit, can live mysteriously within a person's spirit. Couple the power of Christ's presence with His personal fellowship and it is then and only then that it is possible to live correctly and to overcome the difficulties of life. Introducing people to Jesus for change is a whole lot more biblical than trying to change them ourselves.

God makes it quite clear in his Word that he has only one answer to every human need—his Son, Jesus Christ. In all his dealings with us he works by taking *us* out of the way and substituting Christ in our place. The Son of God died instead of us for our forgiveness: he lives instead of us for our deliverance. So we can speak of two substitutions—a Substitute on the Cross who secures our forgiveness and a Substitute within who secures our victory. It will help us greatly, and save us from much confusion, if we keep constantly before us this fact, that God will answer all our questions in one way and one way only, namely, by showing us more of his Son.*

The residency of God's Spirit within the human spirit allowed Paul to declare; "Yet in all these things we are more than conquerors through Him who loved us" (Rom 8:37). Don't miss the intent of this Scripture. Paul is not saying we are more than conquerors in and of ourselves. He is saying that the conquering element works only through Jesus. Paul's understanding of what constituted an overcoming life was in direct correlation with his understanding that he had become a "partaker of the divine nature" (2 Pet 1:2-4). This incredible and profound truth concerning the availability of God's Spirit to live within the human spirit is what fired the early church, setting it ablaze with God's glory. These people had been introduced to all the do's and don'ts ever recorded in history, and they knew that righteousness was not an option in relating to a Holy God. But how to attain right living through a stubborn mind and body was the issue making the Mosaic Law foremost in their minds as the only way to accomplish the task. The Law, however, in as much as it was good in pointing out righteousness, was still a heavy weight. It demanded righteousness but gave no help in obtaining it. Yet, prior to Jesus there was no option. The Law was the only way to God.

Then Jesus! It wasn't that His advent was unexpected, at least for those who understood the Scriptures, it was the way He did things when He got here that confused most people. For centuries the Prophets had told of the coming of a mighty King. But what kind of a King tells you to love your enemies? What kind of compassionate Ruler wants you to give up all you own? Who wants to follow Someone who seems disinterested in Roman oppression and even pays taxes to this corrupt government?

While walking with Jesus, Peter carried his sword ever ready to answer the command to charge against these soldiers of tyranny. If, in those early years, Peter and the rest of the disciples could have raised their eyes a few degrees above the horizon and into the heavenlies they would have seen a war unmatched on earth. An understanding of this war would have easily explained why Jesus did things the way He did. However, not until Christ's mission was complete would they see clearly and be empowered to fight in this kind of war, to fight as it were, "the good fight of faith." Their final clash was to be "against principalities, powers, against the rulers of the darkness of this age, against spiritual *hosts* of wickedness in the heavenly *places*" (Eph 6:12).

Although the disciples understood little about the demonic realm, Jesus was introducing them to this awareness. In the midst of His teachings Jesus promised them "authority to trample on serpents and scorpions, and over all the power of the enemy" (Luke 10:19). He also promised that the works He did they would also do and greater works (See John 14:12). The only thing that hindered fighting such powerful demonic forces was human weakness, the result of separation from God.

Mankind would need, not only Christ's commission, but also the ability and power to carry out His mandates. How could they fight an enemy so superior? How could they come against that which they could not see? The answer was profound, beyond their wildest imagination. If they would allow it to happen, Jesus by His Spirit would live within them. Jesus promised that the Holy Spirit would come to not only walk with them in order to give aid, counsel, and comfort, but that He would live *within* them as well (See John 14:17).

It is only on the basis of the indwelling Christ that anyone has the ability to overcome both the flesh and the devil. That is why we read in so many places in the Bible of this kind of intimacy with Jesus. "I am the vine, you are the branches. He who abides in Me, and I in him, bears much fruit; for without Me you can do nothing" (John 15:5).

Don't Miss The Point

Don't miss the point. We are not creators or even instigators of that which is good, holy, and right. We are participators of the divine nature—the element of God working to bring about the perfection. "For they indeed for a few days chastened *us* as seemed *best* to them, but He for *our* profit, that *we* may be partakers of His holiness" (Heb 12:10).

---

*. Nee, Watchman. *The Normal Christian Life.* Wheaton, IL: Tyndale House Publishers, Inc.; Fort Washington, PA: Christian Literature Crusade, 1957, p.12.

Chapter 3:

Shallow Conversions

The cry of the sinner must always be, "What can I do to rid myself of my offense?" Moral breakdown and other problems within the Body of Christ might easily be traced to a kind of Christianity that fails to deal with sin. We must not miss the mark by placing most of the salvation emphasis on what God will give to those who are His, rather than on a plea for His mercy. The breakdown can also be attributed to a lack of the manifestation of the indwelling Christ. When we do not understand the principle of "partaking of the divine nature," the alternative is to reap the destruction of the flesh.

It is alleged that Christianity sometimes languishes because of lack of commitment, and of attitudes of apathy and self-interest on the part of believers. If the evaluation were true it seems inconceivable that anyone would take lightly the wonder and awe of a life engaged with the Creator of the universe. Yet, not a few Christian leaders groan that it is no small struggle to get people motivated spiritually. One of the major obstacles has to do with those who sit in church on Sunday, but have little further part in the ongoing development of God's Kingdom.

Lack of commitment and apathy, however, may not be the core of the real problem. They may be the effects of much deeper and more profound problems, a kind of tip-of-the-iceberg condition. Some would assert that carnality is the titanic monster of the Church's failures. Certainly, carnality in Christ's Body has always been a problem. The flesh is no easy obstacle for anyone, and life's concerns and basic needs often hinder the pursuit of spiritual life. But no, even carnality has no power when it collides with the Savior.

There have been discussions as to why sports events draw more enthusiasm than meeting with other believers. Do people really get more out of baseball than fellowship? Many seem to in cheering for their favorite team! Leaders find themselves discouraged when a great deal of effort to put a gathering together draws only a handful of the faithful. Others wonder why that for each person entering the front door of their place of worship there is someone exiting through the back. Church increase, although not always a sign of true spiritual growth, is something to be expected when evangelism is at the core of biblical conviction. There is no growth without evangelism.

Then there is this thing called "Consumer Christianity," which is no joke to some leaders who find that sheep wander from one pasture to another at the slightest whim. When tasting and eating replace planting, watering, and tending, there is no harvest. Try building a musical group, training classes, or a youth department when workers become disillusioned, offended, or critical over issues that are microscopic. Try leading people whose personal agendas must have priority if they are to have anything to do with the Body of Christ. Look into your community and you will find numerous people representing some kind of church background, but who no longer attend any kind of fellowship.

Renewal services are often thought to be the solution to these problems. Drum things up and get people excited about serving God. Remind them of their obligations. Show them how they must live if they are to claim true salvation. That way commitment will return and apathy will go away. Those who try this approach usually find that things don't really change that much, and the lasting effects that do take place are minimal.

What, then, are we up against in light of biblical mandates, including building the local church?[1] In short, we are up against shallow Christianity that knows little of being "partakers of the divine nature" (2 Pet 1:4). When Christianity loses its power, it is usually due to participation in self-effort and/or self-indulgence, rather than drawing strength, courage, and righteousness from God.

If Jesus is really the center of the salvation experience and people are given something less, then to what should these people be committed? Unfortunately, we want it to be to our churches. We often ask for commitment to church programs from people who have little, if any, commitment to Jesus. And although, it is very right to work diligently within the local congregation, the commitment to do so must come directly from Christ Himself.

But why little or no commitment on the part of many who appear to be a part of the Kingdom? In some cases it is because they never became aware of the need, and that because they were never confronted with their sin.[2] If Christ is presented only as a way to solve one's problems, we are in danger of never really making a true biblical commitment to Him. And true commitment to Jesus has, for the last two thousand years, always manifested itself in serving the Body of Christ. Instead, the motive to identify with Jesus is based upon what God can do for a person; how He can enhance and make life better. And when times get tough, God gets blamed for not intervening with answers and solutions. Where, then, is commitment? There isn't any!

Was Jesus presented as a Savior from one's problems so that we might enjoy a better life, or as a Savior from sin? Did the salvation message reach one's ears so that he cried, "Sirs, what must I do to be saved?" (Acts 16:30) or was it presented in a way so as not to offend people? Or, maybe not presented at all because it was not understood? Did I come to God because I was away from Him, or because of what He could do for me? The gospel message is not simply the development of a better life. It is one of co-crucifixion with Jesus, the result of which is annihilation, not betterment, of all that represents the "old nature." (See Rom 6:6; Eph 4:22; Col 3:9). Paul spoke of this when he wrote: "I have been crucified with Christ; it is no longer I who live, but Christ lives in me; and the *life* which I now live in the flesh I live by faith in the Son of God, who loved me and gave Himself for me." (Gal 2:20). If any of the previous life, with all of its rebellion and self-love remains, there is no room for Christ. Life in Jesus is not about success. It is about becoming a new person. "New," not just changed. You can put fresh paint on an old car and make it look nice, but it is still not new. (See 2 Cor 5:17)

When the emphasis is on the development of self, even that of talents and abilities, the result is confidence in those talents and abilities. When the emphasis is on Jesus, we develop confidence in Him.

Much of today's preaching represents ten steps to a good marriage, fifteen ways to raise children, or a dozen things to do for some other concern. Technically speaking the material is usually very good and represents biblical truths that need to be taught. The problem is that we are supposed to *do* these things if we are to be successful; and we are right back into *doing* through the power of self-will, which leads to self-righteousness. The message is really about our ability to perform or to follow a program. Where is Jesus in the mix?

Make no mistake, deeds do matter. Obedience *is* relevant. Without holiness no one will see God. Jesus says, "I know your works...." But, again, the issue is, Does righteousness come by self-effort or by "walking in the Spirit?" Am I in tune with Jesus so that His life flows in and through me or do I operate on my own thinking, initiatives, and reason?

---

1. I am aware of the emerging church movement, and yet no matter how the church is defined, any group of God's people in a particular area represent the local Church, including the emerging Church. They will have to deal with the same issues as has any other group of people who have set out to serve Christ. On another note, the Church has always had to "emerge" from times of stagnation. The idea is nothing new.

2. Another reason that commitment to God's Kingdom is minimal in many Christians is the stress and anxiety created by the cares of this life. But, again, we are back to the need for Jesus and for casting our cares on Him (1 Pet 5:7).

Chapter 4:

Prayer: The Development of a Relationship

Prayer is much more than asking God for things. Petition, the element of asking, is only one part of the many aspects of prayer. The subject of unanswered prayer is really one of unanswered petition. In that regard, there is no such thing as unanswered prayer. Petition is only a small part of prayer that seems unanswered.

The Bible is clear on how to establish a relationship with God. Jesus taught that no one comes to the Father, except through Him (John 14:6). The disciples knew well where the path to God began. "There is no other name under heaven, given among men, whereby we must be saved" (Acts 4:12). But relationship has no practical meaning without dialogue. The sharing in friendship and fellowship gives depth and meaning to any accord, even with God.

Once the relationship is established through Jesus, it is then to be nurtured and developed by prayer. This unique and divine way of communicating is meant first and foremost to enhance fellowship with God. It is a discourse over things of mutual interest. Ironically, and erroneously, prayer is most often thought of as a way of getting things *from* God. The average person equates prayer with petition. More than a few have felt a strain in their relationship with Him because they never got beyond a long list of requests. Not that this bothers God to the point of rejecting us, but we sense that this approach is similar to putting quarters in a vending machine. There is something selfish and impersonal about always asking for things.

How backwards we are in our preaching when we tell people that we have an unlimited number of checks to be written on the bank of heaven. The heartbeat of the message should be that we have a God who wants to fellowship with us. If the emphasis is placed first on the things a person can get from God, he or she may miss the intimacy that sparks the understanding that He really cares about the relationship. If we are only concerned with getting answers to petitions, we may miss the fact that He loves us—deeply, passionately, and profoundly.

Earthly parents who give their children an abundance of material goods, but deny them friendship and fellowship, rob them of life's most valuable experiences. Don't miss the point. We can rob ourselves of our most basic need in life— fellowship with God—if petition is allowed to be the central focus of the relationship (See 1 Cor 1:9).

Everything about the creation of a human being was meant for community—first with God and second with others. Concerning people, the Bible is specific on the need for fellowshipping with one another. "And let us consider one another in order to stir up love and good works, not forsaking the assembling of ourselves together, as *is* the manner of some, but exhorting *one another*" (Heb 10:24-25 Italics added). Those who draw away from others, both physically and/or emotionally, cannot experience the wonder and fulfillment found in relationships. To withdraw opens the door to loneliness and feelings of rejection. The same is true with God. We were meant for fellowship with Him as well, and prayer is the means for accomplishing that goal.

Prayer keeps Christ's life flowing within us. Think of His life as a beam of light or a running stream. His eternal life, then, is the flowing of His life in us. Eternal life is not a state of "being" as much as it is the affect of a relationship. Because Christ's Spirit lives in us, we have eternal life both now and in eternity.

That we were created for God is testified to not only by the Scriptures, but also by the lack of satisfaction in everything else we look to for fulfillment. The availability of God's presence for which the human heart longs, delights the soul and transforms the person. It is this "Presence" that accomplishes the righteousness of the Law. It is this "Presence" for which we were made.

Intimacy with God is lost when prayer is mostly mechanical, the fulfillment of an obligation necessary to appease God. You may never know how much a man knows of God by his prayer, but often you can tell how much he doesn't know. Human character is no doubt determined more by who we hang around with than by any other factor. In a similar manner men and women who associate with God tend to develop characteristics in line with His nature— compassion, patience, honesty, loyalty, reliability, and uprightness. Don't miss the point! Try to develop any of these virtues on your own and the result is generally a self-righteousness that does more damage than good.

William Penn wrote of George Fox, "But above all he excelled in prayer. The inwardness and weight of his spirit, the reverence and solemnity of his address and behavior, and the fewness and fullness of his words have often struck even strangers with admiration as they used to reach others with consolation. The most awful, living, reverend frame I ever felt or beheld, I must say, was his prayer. And truly it was a testimony. He knew and lived nearer to the Lord than other men, for they that know him most will see most reason to approach him with reverence and fear."

Should Fox's testimony or that of any other like him touch your heart so that you could easily desire to be such a person, know that these great people did not make themselves into greatness. God made them into who they became out of intimacy with Himself. Greatness of character cannot be imitated; it must be developed through fellowship.

In a previous era it was preached that those who would be fearless, compassionate, and powerful men and women of God, seeking to separate themselves from all that ruins, corrupts, and disqualifies, must be first of all praying people. Nothing has changed. Only in prayer do we become what we are to be in spirit and authority before the world and Satan's demons. It must never be thought, however, that we are to make ourselves pious, devoted, and consecrated people of God before we actually come to Him. It is in nearness to the King that we become like Him. Only in His presence does one find the character he seeks. It is not found somewhere deeply imbedded in the human frame to be retrieved by meditation or any other form of contemplation or introspection. It is found in Him alone.

Another element of prayer is the concept of deputization, similar to that of a police officer being deputized. "The works that I do," Jesus said, "you will do and greater" (John 14:12). God's purpose is to extend His authority on earth through those who identify with Him. His desire is that we do the works that He did. For as incredible as this may sound, it is still the substance of Scripture. "I give you authority to trample on serpents and scorpions and over all the power of the enemy" (Luke 10:19). But this feature must be understood to go hand and hand with the fact that without Him we can do nothing (John 15:5). In that light there is the need to be in constant contact with Jesus. Without some kind of bond of which prayer is the connection, we have no ability to repel the forces of evil. A man without a prayer life is no more capable of winning victories than a baseball player is without a bat.

Most Christians will tell you that prayer is important to spiritual life, but that still doesn't mean that it is easy to pray. It is not easy to give up interest in myself in order to concentrate on Someone else. To call on God is to acknowledge that I am not God.

Prayer has other hindrances—a wandering mind, weariness, busyness, laziness, etc.—it also has the problem of trying to figure out what to say. At this point God offers some encouragement. In Romans 8:26, He basically declares, "Don't worry about it, just come and I'll get things started." Along these lines Charles Spurgeon maintained, "Prayer itself is an art which only the Holy Spirit can teach us. He is the giver of all prayer. Pray for prayer—pray till you can pray."

Chapter 5:

A Bid to Justify the Flesh

It is easy to want to justify sin on the basis of weak flesh, but nowhere does Scripture excuse delinquent behavior. Not only are we to deny the flesh, we are to crucify it. God's great grace must never be used to rationalize sin.

F.J. Huegel points us to the questions that plague those whose bid for righteousness hangs perilously on the precipice of failure: "Why does not the Savior, so tender and so understanding, so loving and so wise, not make requirements more in keeping with human nature? Why does He seem to be so unreasonable? Why does He not demand of us what we might reasonably attain? He bids us soar, but we have no wings."*

Walk with Jesus but for a short while and we are confronted with the responsibilities of loving our enemies, praying without ceasing, denying ourselves, rejoicing always, giving no place to the flesh, resisting the devil, thinking pure thoughts, and a further array of mandates, all part of this new Kingdom of light and life. If the gulf between our abilities and God's expectations were not so expansive, we could more easily celebrate a victorious life. Yet, the gulf exists. We are light years away from the holiness of a Holy God. Regardless, the commandment remains: we are to be holy as He is Holy (1 Pet 1:16). Literally, we are to be perfect.

It is at this point that human reasoning, and sometimes theology, goes awry. Human thinking claims Christian

36

principles to be ideals to consider, but not standards we are expected to attain. If it is not the attitude that, "I'm as good as anybody," then it's the, "God knows that I'm weak" syndrome and assumes that weakness excuses right living. Sometimes errant theology makes a similar proposal by asserting that God's grace cancels inappropriate behavior. All a person needs to do is be sorry for the things he or she does wrong. But the Scriptures cut cross-grain to this argument. "Shall we continue in sin that grace may abound?" Paul asks. "Certainly not!" he responds (Rom 6:1-2). Later, he emphatically states, "Sin shall not have dominion over you." "Likewise you also, reckon yourselves to be dead indeed to sin, but alive to God in Christ Jesus our Lord" (Rom 6:11). "And those *who are* Christ's have crucified the flesh with its passions and desires. If we live in the Spirit, let us also walk in the Spirit. Let us not become conceited, provoking one another, envying one another" (Gal 5:24-26). God's grace wasn't meant to excuse sin, it was meant to deal with it.

There is not one of us who in looking at the obligations of the Old and New Testaments isn't at times tempted to despair. But allowing the commandments to slip from our minds, either by way of preoccupation with the cares of this life, or for reasons of weakness seems to lessen the pain of guilt. In this way we are not faced with the dilemma of reaching what appears to be the unattainable.

Many of the commandments are so far beyond the abilities of the natural man to perform that either Christ was speaking idealistic or He was speaking to a special group of people of which few were meant to be a part. The glare of righteousness causes many to turn from the presence of the Lord. "Then they said to Moses, 'You speak with us, and we will hear; but let not God speak with us, lest we die'" (Ex 20:19).

There is another way in which the flesh attempts to deal with the requirements of Christ. Dedication, devotion, and involvement in spiritual things are easily used to justify weakness. "How could God possibly be upset with my idiosyncrasies and shortcomings in light of all that I do for Him? After all, I've sacrificed time, energy, and money to work in His Kingdom. Certainly that must count for something." Nor is the problem of holiness and righteousness lessened by an ultra disciplined approach to following Jesus' commands. Sheer will power, which often covers up the flesh, proposes to bring about holiness. A man may never steal, cheat, lie, or commit adultery by his own ability to constrain himself, and still miss the mark.

What is the mark? Jesus! It is literally, Christ living in us. Therefore, let not Jesus be regarded only as the Savior. He is also the head of the Body, the Captain of God's army, the Groom preparing to receive His bride, and the only Source for separation from the flesh and the devil. That's the story—only Jesus can deliver from sin; from its presence, power, and penalty. To do so He must communicate with His people. This He does through His Word and deep within the recesses of the human spirit.

I do not want to minimize someone's personal pain at this point. Who of God's people has not questioned, while in a valley of despair, whether or not God had cast us off because of our failures? Who has not probed to find whether or not some undetected sin had made heaven so silent? But the journey soon revealed that we had not been abandoned.

Will, then, we settle for less then a full redemption, especially in light of the Scriptures that teach that He came to deliver us from sin in this present life, not just in eternity? "And she will bring forth a Son, and you shall call His name JESUS, for He will **save His people from their sins**" (Mat 1:21).

Will we justify our sin, only to be brought under its power? The disciples knew well that Jesus gave us the right and ability to live in righteousness. Peter wrote of Christ, "Who Himself bore our sins in His own body on the tree, that we, having died to sins, might live for righteousness" (2 Pet 2:24).

Paul taught that the new man in Christ was created "in true righteousness and holiness." "That you put off, concerning your former conduct, the old man which grows corrupt according to the deceitful lusts, and be renewed in the spirit of your mind, and that you put on the new man which was created according to God, in true righteousness and holiness" (Eph 4:22-23).

The early church understood that Jesus was sent to turn people away from sin, "To you first, God, having raised up His Servant Jesus, sent Him to bless you, in turning away every one *of you* from your iniquities" (Acts 3:26).

John the Baptist's father, Zacharias, prophesied of the manner in which we were to serve God, "To grant us that we, being delivered from the hand of our enemies, might serve Him without fear, in holiness and righteousness before Him all the days of our life" (Luke 1:74-75).

God looks at the church, His Body, in a unique way, "That He might present her to Himself a glorious church, not having spot or wrinkle or any such thing, but **that she**

should be holy and without blemish" (Eph 5:27). In light of these and other similar Scriptures one thing is clear, God wants sin removed from our lives in this life, and not just in eternity.

There is a thought that carries a great deal of truth, but can be abused. It is that "positionally" we are seated with Christ in the heavenlies, but practically we are still here on earth. The idea is that we possess all the fullness of what God has for us as His people right now, but that realizing that may not happen here on earth. Certainly, there are things that we will not experience until we are with Jesus. At the same time, we may miss God's intent for His Church at this time by not appropriating truths that are meant for us today. For instance, Jesus commissioned His disciples, including you and me, with authority over demons (Luke 10:19). We don't have to be bound by their influence. If Jesus says the works that I do, a believer has the ability to do also, and even greater works, then why stay burdened and even oppressed? Why not seek God for His guidance in using His power to do miracles? "Most assuredly, I say to you, he who believes in Me, the works that I do he will do also; and greater *works* than these he will do, because I go to My Father" (John 14:12).

To say that because of weak flesh we have to wait until heaven before we are delivered from sin is to misunderstand the indwelling Holy Spirit. It is true that here on earth we will always wrestle with sin and, at times, need to go to God for forgiveness. But the truth still remains that with "Christ in me" I have hope for release from the power of sin now. "For if by one man's offense death reigned through the one, much more those who receive abundance of grace and of the gift of righteousness **will reign in life** through the One, Jesus Christ" (Rom 5:17).

---

*. Huegel, F.J. *Bone of His Bone*. Grand Rapids, MI. Zondervan Publishing House. 1940. p.16.

Chapter 6:

Sovereignty and Free Will

How much does God want us to exercise the free will He has given us? How much does He want to be engaged directly in human affairs? Does human free will determine the outcome of a life, or does God's sovereignty determine it alone, or is it a combination of both?

There are, perhaps, no greater issues surrounding theology and how to live life, than that of trying to understand how the human "will" operates in view of God's sovereignty. How much does God want to be involved in my life? Or, does He simply want to leave me with mandates on how to live (commandments) and wait to see how well I do? When it comes to believing Him for things, am I supposed to do nothing until He does something, or do I do as much as I can, leaving the outcome up to Him? In marriage, should I look for a spouse or expect that He will bring me one? Should I look for a job or expect that the phone will ring with an offer? You will probably find as many opinions on the subject as people you ask; all of them falling at various places between what appears to be opposite ends of a very wide spectrum.

The matter is obviously complex. On the sovereignty side, because of the belief that nothing in life happens outside of God's will, some extrapolate this to the point that they are afraid to do anything for fear of doing something that might bump up against His indomitable will. Some go so far as to form a fatalistic mind-set that puts forth little effort for either spiritual or natural development, simply because they believe that no one can change what God has pre-determined. They believe He has prearranged everything. This extreme can cause a passive approach to life, something very dangerous to spiritual life.

On the free will side there is the position (in its extreme) that God delivers the commands and we go about obeying them, at least we try to do so to the best of our ability. In this case God seems to be saying, Here is what needs to take place, get busy and make it happen. At this point all moral government rests solely on human shoulders. Some assume that all that God wants is obedience and that obeying is entirely up to us. Out of this kind of thinking Christianity easily deteriorates into hoop jumping, and like one young lady asked, "If I miss a hoop, do I have to start all over again?" This extreme often causes anxiety and despair in those who wonder if they are ever doing enough to please God.

To conclude that sovereignty and free will should have some kind of balance point is one thing, but to see it worked out is quite another. Who doesn't vacillate between trying to figure out what we are to do, and what we are to leave in God's hands.

Free will does not threaten God. To be *in* control of everything does not mean that He chooses *to* control everything.

Approaching this problem of free will and sovereignty should not be a matter of choosing one side over the other. There are sufficient Scriptures to indicate that both sides, minus the extremes, are correct at the same time. They appear to be simply opposite sides of the same coin.

Someone has adequately summed up this dualistic approach to living with the statement, "Without God, man cannot. Without man, God will not." The issue is cooperation, of which the devil and his demons lose their influence when man is reconciled to God and goes about working with Him for restoration.

Consider it this way. First, God gives the directions for living. They are, for the most part, parameters for operating successfully in this world. They are for using things correctly according to the manner in which they were made. The matter at this point is not in "doing," but first in becoming "willing to do what is right." For in doing we immediately find ourselves bewildered for lack of ability. Our success in pleasing God by obeying Him is not determined by our ability to perform, but by our willingness to get involved. The human will is the issue. If ability were the object, there would be no indictment against human strength. Shame alone testifies to our weak condition. The broad-based reality of human failure begins in Genesis and continues through Revelation. "For I know that in me (that is, in my flesh) nothing good dwells" (Rom 7:18). We must not underestimate the importance of human free will. Fenelon observed, "The will to love God is the whole of religion."

No person, in his or her condition outside of Jesus, is capable of obeying God's commands. But God in His grace only lets us partially off the hook. We remain responsible for our condition, along with our actions and attitudes. His favor toward us, however, allows that He will make up for the shortfall in strength and abilities. You can tell a four year old all day long to clean his room. In most cases very little, if anything, will happen. But get down beside him and help him and the job eventually gets done. That's very close to how God works.

If God proposes to make up for whatever shortcomings we have, then we have no excuse for living outside of a life of faith and holiness. If He is willing to help me clean my room, there are unlimited possibilities in a relationship with Him.

When a person fails to live in this truth, it is often because he has not come into this understanding. And sadly, "My people perish for lack of knowledge" (Hos 4:6). But this is not a hidden matter. The simplicity and forthrightness of Philippians 2:13 points directly to this truth, "For it is God who works in you both to will and to do for His good pleasure."

Just the realization that God knows our weaknesses and is willing to help in overcoming them, gives great courage to those who have made up their minds to, not only worship and serve Him, but to live a life of holiness and righteousness before Him as well.

Again, if we are not resting in Jesus and relying upon His help and strength, we often struggle wondering if we are doing enough, or if we have done something wrong when some difficulty arises.

Don't miss the point. The clay can't mold itself. We can only agree to be molded. Our hope is in the potter's hands.

Chapter 7:

First Love Rejected

No person will ever attain righteousness outside of an understanding of God's love. No one will ever experience holiness until he or she has opened up to that love.

Chapter Two of the book of Revelation contains Christ's evaluation of seven churches in Asia Minor. Six of these churches find themselves the focal point of His anger. Should Jesus seem harsh in His assessment, one must understand that His displeasure is preceded by His Calvary sacrifice, a measure of amazing love and incredible concern.

It is to the church at Ephesus that He directs a concern about their love. The issue was that they had left their first love. "First love" is the astonishing element of the beginning of the regeneration process. Most Christians experience it at conversion. It is that unique sense that heaven has reached down and touched them. For the Ephesians, that love had withered and died. That which John says had come as a result of God's love ("We love Him because He first loved us" 1 John 10:19) had ceased. The implication is that something had replaced His love. Jesus isn't probing to engender guilt in hopes that they will try harder to love Him. Neither is He challenging them as if to say, "Why don't you love me anymore, especially after all I've done for you?" Christ's confrontation with the church is over lost fellowship, as well as honor and respect. "Why have you neglected our relationship? Why do you fail to allow me to show you my love?" Similar words were spoken centuries before when God asked Adam, "Where are you?" This was not a question of geography. God's divine GPS system had not malfunctioned. It was a question of what Adam was doing to destroy the intimacy of the relationship. Any time a person walks away from God he is walking away from Someone who cares. Hannah Whitall Smith wrote, "He is our Father, and He loves us, and He knows just what is best, and therefore, of course, His will is the very most blessed thing that can come to us under any circumstances."[1]

First love sanctifies a relationship in such a way that nothing matters but the other person. It is not difficult to please that person, but rather joyous. "For this is the love of God, that we keep His commandments. And His commandments are not burdensome (1 John 5:3). The Christian experience is on shaky ground anytime obligation replaces an enthusiastic approach to loving Jesus. In the minds of most Christians are rules and regulations rather than love in approaching a relationship with God.

Christ knew that rules, and especially the Law (not the righteousness of the Law) in its unrelenting demands, had the power to supplant His love. This is why Paul reproved the Galatians for returning to the Law for righteousness. "Did you receive the Spirit by the works of the law, or by the hearing of faith? Are you so foolish? Having begun in the Spirit, are you now being made perfect by the flesh? (Gal 3:2-3). "Therefore by the deeds of the law no flesh will be justified in His sight, for by the law *is* the knowledge of sin. But now the righteousness of God apart from the law is revealed, being witnessed by the Law and the Prophets, even the righteousness of God *which is* through faith in Jesus Christ to all and on all who believe...." (Rom 3:20-22).

If a person is taught to live a specified lifestyle outside of God's immediate help, and proceeds to try to live righteously according to his or her own strengths and capabilities, all of their energy is consumed in performance. It doesn't take long for a person to wear out by trying to be good. Christianity from this perspective soon deteriorates into a very hard to live life. Along the way it picks up immeasurable amounts of guilt, condemnation, and shame.

We can rally our own abilities all day long and get nowhere. At this point self-righteousness becomes easier to understand when viewed in the light of self-effort. In that light all of us have differing degrees of self-righteousness, and not just those who act with some sort of arrogance.

Courage is quickly lost when responsibility for righteousness rests solely on our own shoulders. We came to Christ 'out of control' and will remain that way if we are expected to simply pick ourselves up and learn to do better. A person will bend a railroad girder faster than he will turn his own flesh into submission to the righteous demands of God. That is why the Scriptures are so explicit on the need for God's righteousness. "But of Him you are in Christ Jesus, who became for us wisdom from God—and righteousness[2] and sanctification and redemption—that, as it is written, *"He who glories, let him glory in the Lord"* (1 Cor 1:30). "For He made Him who knew no sin to *be* sin for us, that we might become the righteousness of God in Him" (2 Cor 5:21). "For if righteousness *comes* through the law, then Christ died in vain" (Gal 2:21). "Is the law then against the promises of God? Certainly not! For if there had been a law given which could have given life, truly righteousness would have been by the law. But the Scripture has confined all under sin, that the promise by faith in Jesus Christ might be given to those who believe. But before faith came, we were kept under guard by the law, kept for the faith, which would afterward be revealed. Therefore the law was our tutor *to bring us* to Christ, that we might be justified by faith. But after faith has come, we are no longer under a tutor" (Gal 3:21-25).

Don't miss the point. The Law (rules and regulations) was to "bring us" to Christ. What does that mean? It means that God wants a relationship that is so intimate that a believer lives directly within the constant presence and influence of Jesus. "For what the law could not do in that it was weak through the flesh, God did by sending His own Son…." (Rom 8:3). Try to live holy and righteous outside of Jesus and you are only kidding yourself. But live "in" Jesus and you find His strength to overcome. It is precisely His life working in us that creates the element of love—that which the Ephesian church had lost. His love and strength is what fulfills the righteousness of the Law.

The Psalmist knew well the powerful change that takes place from the smallest whisper of Christ's Spirit within the human heart, "Your gentleness has made me great" (Psa 18:35). He experienced God's intimacy through the language of the Spirit.

Anyone living under a cloud of commands, still hoping to do enough to please God, is missing the most important element of the Christian faith. Many view a God sitting in heaven with a divine scorecard waiting to see how well a person is going to do.

Certainly, God is pleased with righteousness. It is a requirement in His Kingdom. But He is not pleased when a person tries to dig it out of his or her own personal treasury of goodness. Either you get righteousness from Him or you don't get it at all.

For many people, it seems easier to try to do well and justify failure than it is to seek God for His righteousness. Few take the time to find Him in His Word and prayer. The cares of life and general laziness put off the pursuit of God until some disaster touches our lives. Even then we are reluctant to run wholeheartedly to Him, especially when we begin to feel a little relief from the trauma of the moment. But the only solution to becoming the person God created us to be is to allow Jesus to change us.

---

1. Hannah Whitall Smith. *The Christian's Secret of a Happy Life*. New York: Fleming Revel Company, MCMLII. p.47.
2. The word "righteousness" in these passages has been underlined for emphasis.

Chapter 8:

Source and Inspiration Rather than Model or Pattern

When a person is looked up to as either a model or pattern, there is often great difficulty in becoming like that person due to human weakness. Trying to live to the example of Jesus is not only impossible it is terribly discouraging.

An amazing amount of self-righteousness continues to exist even after a person comes to Christ. Few would debate the subject in light of our need to mature. That Christianity is a process is evident from the convicting spotlight of the Holy Spirit in His unrelenting work to deal with the human condition of self. But sometimes change gets stuck on elements of false or misleading theologies. Sometimes we miss great truths by a simple perception that is close to being correct, but do not embrace a full measure. Consider the idea that Jesus is our model and pattern for living. True? Yes! Well, not so fast. There is more to the statement than meets the eye. Certainly, and without question, Jesus is the perfect example of a man, and we are to be like Him in righteousness and character.

But when Jesus is looked upon as either model or pattern the tendency is to set Him up as the ideal for which we are to strive. On the surface that sounds correct, but it doesn't take long and the question is whether or not we were ever meant to be Christ-like in this life. The sheer impossibility of the task takes its toll and we are prone to change our minds and settle for less. "Yes," we may believe, "Christ is the model of perfection and I am to be like Him, but ...." From here it is easy to justify the failure of living far below the measure of His life. And so we use illegitimate statements to ease the guilt. "I'm not perfect, just forgiven."

The model and pattern idea is found in most other religions of the world. By following the principles, decrees, and lifestyles of men such as Mohammed, Confucius, or Buddha, the goal is to reach their state of spirituality. The desired affect is to achieve likeness or similarity based on hard work. There is great appeal to some when the promise is that of reward for accomplishment.

Self-righteousness is attractive in any religion, especially when it promises personal gain. Although Christianity offers the greatest gain in this life and in eternity, God's offer has always been the development of a relationship with Jesus and not just future benefits either on earth or in heaven. He wants to give us Jesus, not just what Jesus can do for us.

If the Bible were first and foremost a book on how to live, it would have said far less about Jesus. Read it carefully and it turns out to be a Book about Him and how a relationship with Him produces the desired affect of righteousness. It is within this framework of relationship and fellowship that strength for right living is imparted. Thus, Jesus becomes our source and inspiration for pleasing God. View Him as model and pattern and He remains distant and unapproachable. Allowed to be one's source and inspiration He becomes personal and close. This is not a matter of semantics; it is biblical truth that must not be missed if we are to understand Jesus. View Jesus as kind, merciful, and patient and then try to live these and other positive characteristics and failure is around the corner. View these as impossible traits but necessary for righteous living and call upon Jesus for help in fulfilling them, and success is imminent. *"With God*, all things are possible (Mat 19:26)."

To have some idea of what constitutes right living, and then to persistently and consistently fail to live that way produces considerable amounts of frustration and confusion, conditions for which the human soul is prone to react, but not always with positive results. The roadside of spiritual life is littered with the remains of those who have failed to stay on track and have consequently collapsed under the weight of discouragement.

If the Bible expected right living to be a consequence of personal ability, the issue of failure would not be as widespread as it is, literally encompassing the entire human race. The biblical assessment is that all our righteousness is like filthy rags (Isa 64:6). Our condition is regretful at best. God's assessment, however, was never meant to condemn any more than a person is condemning a car by telling its owner that it has a flat tire. The issue is that something is wrong and needs fixing. And Jesus is saying, *Let Me help.*

Chapter 9:

Those Who Turn Back

While salvation may be a free gift, few would argue that Christianity is an easy life to live. On the other hand, many who once lived for self and Satan would argue that it is easier and better to live for Jesus. If that is really true, then why do so many turn away from the Savior? Why do people go back into the world?

If Jesus is Who He says He is, and if He is the only way to the Father, then salvation through Him is of utmost importance. This is why the Church is to be a missionary and evangelism organism. But seeing people find Christ is only part of the challenge. The other part is seeing them continue with Him and not turn back. The reality, however, is that there are countless numbers of people who once served Jesus, but for one reason or another do not do so today.

In Christian leadership, this should be a major concern. Why is it that many go back into the world after a time with the Savior? What is there of the old life that could possibly draw a person away from the King? The answers are not easy, but there are things to consider in today's Church that, if corrected, would certainly minimize the potential for numbers of people from going back into the world.

To understand why some people give up and quit serving God it is important to understand the true nature of Christianity. Again, as stated earlier, most people see Christianity as a list of commands, a list of do's and don'ts that are the defining acts of what they think is necessary to make a person a Christian. Some believe that holiness and righteousness characterize the orders of a God Who waits for them to reach a level of perfection. They perceive life as a proving ground to develop the characteristics of one who is worthy of heaven. Certainly, we must agree with the Scriptures that holiness and righteousness are necessary for a person to enter God's presence. The problem: We are incapable of anything that even remotely resembles a lifestyle that would please God. Let me state it again, "For all of our righteousness is as but filthy rags" (Isa 64:6). "There is none righteous, no not one" (Rom 3:10). These Scriptures are not meant to condemn. They exist as an analysis of a condition. They point to the need for something from God, rather than something from us. With an understanding of this human condition, the Psalmist wrote, "My goodness is nothing apart from you" (Psa 16:2). T. Austin Sparks writes:

> "But do not forget that if we mean business with the Holy Spirit, He is not going to allow us to be deceived. I mean that the Holy Spirit is going to expose our true selves. He is going to uncover us and show us thoroughly there is nothing sound in us, nothing to be relied upon in us, in order that He may make it equally clear that it is only in Christ, God's Son, that there is security, and safety and life."[1]

Many of us come to Christ with great enthusiasm only to stagnate at the demands of our new life. Most will affirm that God's decrees are good and necessary for a sound life. But how to perform correctly escapes us, until we like the great Apostle, cry, "I know what's right, but I can't seem to do it. And I know the things that are wrong, but to my disgust, I always find myself doing them" (Rom 7:19 Paraphrased). This is precisely why Paul proclaimed, "Oh wretched man that I am, who will deliver me from this mess?" (Rom 7:24 Paraphrased). And it is one of the reasons why some people give up and quit. After all, continual failure only produces guilt and condemnation. The only hope for some is to stay away from that which reminds them of their spiritual bankruptcy, and that often includes fellowship with other Christians.

That our guilt is real is not the question. We know that we are wrong. No one has to say much to remind us of a life that is both embarrassing and discouraging. To make things worse, some who are hurting find no shortage of other people who continue to make the point that they need to change or face the consequences. Repeated failure certainly doesn't encourage anyone to stay with the program. Eventually, it is easier to develop an eye for something else.[2]

Paul's analysis of his dilemma in the flesh leads us to God's answer to the problem. Paul ends Romans chapter seven with a rather frank, matter-of-fact this is "the answer," as if to say, this has turned out far easier than anyone would have imagined. The solution?—Simply and profoundly, "Jesus." He is saying once again that the gospel message is about Jesus living and working inside of us. It is this knowledge that leads a person into the true Christian experience. Don't miss the point. I don't have to continue in the things I know are wrong, and I can start doing the things I know are right to do, but only as I cooperate with Jesus by His Spirit living in me.

1. Sparks, T. Austin. *The School of Christ.* Lindale, TX; World Challenge, Inc. p.27.

Don't Miss The Point

2. This of course is only one reason why people turn back. Others do so because the world is more attractive or because they refuse the headship of Jesus. Also, see Matthew 13:1-23.

Chapter 10:

Circumstances and Peace of Mind

We were born into a world where, for the most part, circumstances govern our peace of mind. God's plan is to transfer us into a Kingdom where Jesus is our peace.

In the early 1980's a British Airways 747 flying near Jakarta unknowingly flew into a plume of ash from a volcanic eruption. The plane lost power in all four engines and began to descend rapidly on a glide path with an uncertain future. During the suspense a passenger later reported a personal desire for the plane to hurry up and crash and end the terror involved in waiting. Immediate death was more appealing than the tension from not knowing what was going to happen.

Circumstances have a way of determining peace of mind or the lack of it. When things go well we feel secure and safe. When difficulties arise and especially when they are sustained for a period of time we commonly unravel mentally. Fear decommissions peace of mind. Worry builds emotional apprehension. And anxiety opens the door to panic attacks. If the difficult circumstance could be controlled, anxiety would be of little concern. But troubles come as readily as the "sparks from a fire fly upward" (Job 5:7 Paraphrased). And for many of us there isn't much we can do on our own about the resulting emotional devastation.

People deal with pain in various ways. Some seek counsel while others clam up and try to wrestle through it on their own. Some turn to the occult—to palm reading, crystal balls, and tarot cards in hopes of getting a positive word about the future. An increasing number of people try drugs, both legal and illegal, to help cope. Others hope for help by going to church.

Most of us who go through difficult and trying times usually don't look back once the circumstances improve. Not many stop to wonder about what just happened, and then to question how to prevent similar pain in the future. The hope is that it will never happen again, so just go on with your life. But no matter where we live, who we are, or what we do, difficulties come once again and peace of mind dissipates. This is pretty much the scenario as long as peace of mind is attached to circumstances. When circumstances are connected directly to Jesus because we have given them to Him, and have moved into His peace, and His peace has moved into us, circumstances have a lessened affect on our lives. Christ not only gives us peace, He is our peace in a similar way that a parent becomes a child's peace (Eph 2:14). "Peace I leave with you, /My peace I give to you. Let not your heart be troubled, neither let it be afraid" (John 14:27). But notice again, this is not possible outside of a personal and intimate relationship with Him.

God approaches peace in yet another way. He calls it rest. "There remains therefore a rest for the people of God. For he who has entered His rest has himself also ceased from his works as God did from His" (Heb 4:9-10). This rest (from works as a way to salvation) does not mean an absence of difficulty, but rather a deep assurance from Jesus that He is there in the midst of our hurt and pain. Nor does it mean that rest is the same as passivity. To rest (and trust) doesn't mean that I don't look for a job when I'm without one, that I don't seek counsel for direction, that I don't do everything I know to do to spread the gospel. It means that in the midst of moving forward, I allow and appropriate God's peace in my heart.

This mentality is affirmed in numbers of Scriptures. "Casting all your care upon Him, for He cares for you" (1 Pet 5:7). "Therefore do not worry about tomorrow, for tomorrow will worry about its own things. Sufficient for the day *is* its own trouble" (Mat 6:34). "And we know that all things work together for good to those who love God, to those who are the called according to His purpose" (Rom 8:28). "Trust in the Lord with all your heart, /And lean not on your own understanding; In all your ways acknowledge Him, And He shall direct your paths" (Pro 3:5-6).

On what, perhaps, seemed like a normal day, Jesus and His disciples got into a boat and set out to sea. Suddenly a fierce storm arose. The disciples fearing for their lives went to Jesus who was fast asleep in the stern. Awakening, He spoke to the wind and the waves and told them to cease. Don't miss the point. The miracle was not just in the calming of the sea. The real miracle was that the Master of the sea was in the boat.

Chapter 11:

What Would Jesus Do?

We must not deceive ourselves into believing that we have the strength and ability to imitate Jesus. In the same way that a lamb cannot live the life of a lion, we are not capable in ourselves of living like Jesus.

They were a fad, literally a rage for a while. They were the letters WWJD and worn on wristbands and a variety of clothing. They posed a question with the hope that it would trigger a positive response in the midst of temptation and other trying circumstances. These four letters were to remind a person of his or her responsibility to act with honesty, integrity, and moral purity in light of their commitment to Jesus. The question?—What Would Jesus Do?

I don't see them anymore, but wish I did. It would be good for those who still have these reminders imprinted on some wearable item, to dig them out of drawers and closets and to occasionally adorn them once again. In doing so, however, it might be good to first examine some thoughts behind those alphabetic symbols.

"What would Jesus do?" is a wonderful reminder of the need to make positive biblical choices in every aspect of life. Historically, to choose the good and shun the evil has proven itself over and over again to be the only way to experience the best in life. But agreeing with what is right is one thing, while doing it is quite another. To discover the "Jesus way" doesn't always mean that walking in it is going to be easy.

Paul wrote, "To will is present with me...." (Rom 7:18), but accomplishing good intentions can be difficult.

The gap between the desire to do good and actually doing it is often immensely wide. The resulting inner struggle becomes intense. There is something about the soul realm that impinges upon the spirit, creating a fierce internal battle. The warfare, in and of itself, is enough to cause many to give up. We would rather not fight than to do so and always seem to loose.

What would Jesus do? Of course He would do what is right. And He wouldn't fail at it. Why? Because He's the sinless Son of God (Heb 4:15). That is certainly not a statement we can make—we cannot say we are sinless. And weak flesh is simply not strong enough to always succeed in doing right. We've learned by experience that failure is a fundamental aspect of life. Guilt, shame, and condemnation ratify our condition.

If these things are true, it seems a bit ludicrous that we, in our weakness, should attempt to be like Him in His strength? That sounds like a formula for failure? How can one whose personal righteousness, as deplorable as it is, think that he will imitate Christ? But the Scriptures make no provision for the flesh. We are to be holy as He is holy (1 Pet 1:16). "Without holiness no man shall see God" (Heb 12:20).

Yet, there is hope. The Psalmist, David, well understood the road to holiness. Listen to him for a moment to get the picture:

"Wait on the LORD; /Be of good courage, /And He shall strengthen your heart; /Wait, I say, on the LORD!" (Psa 27:14).

"The LORD *is* my strength and my shield; /My heart trusted in Him, and I am helped; /Therefore my heart greatly rejoices, /And with my song I will praise Him" (Psa 28:7).

"The LORD will give strength to His people; /The LORD will bless His people with peace" (Psa 29:11).

"For You *are* my rock and my fortress; /Therefore, for Your name's sake, /Lead me and guide me. Pull me out of the net which they have secretly laid for me, /For You *are* my strength" (Psa 31:3-4).

Did you get it? Don't miss it. David's ability to overcome was not based on his own personal strength. He found that, by spending time waiting on God, he was renewed in spirit by God's Spirit. This refreshing gave him what he needed in order to succeed.

"What would Jesus do?" The thought is still good. It reminds us that standards are involved in holiness and righteousness. Right living is not an option. Lives are ruined in the presence of sin. But I still need to be close to Him if I am to be like Him. And, just as much, I need His help to do what is right.

Chapter 12:

Following Jesus or Walking in the Spirit

The concept of "following" Jesus may have been more for the early disciples than for Christians today. Those who followed Jesus before He returned to the Father did not have the Holy Spirit abiding within, as they soon would receive on the day of Pentecost. After that, the motivation for living would come from within rather than from without.

A common theme among Christians has to do with the idea of following Jesus. The thought is expressed in sermons, books, and songs about faithful people moving forward in the steps of the Master. The book, *In His Steps*[1], along with the lyrics of an old song, "I'm following Jesus—One step at a time..."[2] convey the thinking. The idea, perhaps, comes largely from Christ's words to His original disciples, "Follow Me, and I will **make** you fishers of men" (Mat 4:19). Men and women of various backgrounds left what they were doing to follow Jesus, similar to a soldier following his commander. Days, weeks, and months were given to physically pursuing this unique individual Who had come into their lives. He took many of them wherever He went. He taught them, trained them, and sent them out to do His bidding. He **made** them who they eventually became.

Wars, religious movements, political factions, the entertainment world, all have their celebrated leaders, quite often with a band of enthusiastic followers. To get things done, some must lead while others must follow. That is the natural procedure for government, family, business, and warfare. The concept seems evident and self-explanatory. Both secular and biblical history affirm the process. Even in church government Christ has given apostles, prophets, evangelists, pastors, and teachers (Eph 4:11) as leaders with directions that the rest of His Body follow them as His representatives here on earth (Also see Heb 13:17).

The idea of following has the connotation of replication, of doing the things we see others do. Paul affirmed that this was good when he exhorted, "Imitate me, just as I also *imitate* Christ" (1 Cor 11:1). Imitation is biblical in as much as it is understood to be a design to show the finished product, but not in the idea of a strenuous lifestyle to accomplish the goal. This is where Christianity easily breaks down. We look at the ideal and make arrangements to wind up there by way of anything and everything we can do to force the body and mind into a particular lifestyle. Insufficient strength, ability, and even desire generally ruin the desired result. Consequently, we are back to guilt, condemnation, shame, or in many cases a focus on something else that produces less emotional stress.

This is, perhaps, why little is said in the Scriptures about following Jesus after He ascended into heaven. As I have already said, the very clear and distinct message from this point on was that the Holy Spirit would come, not only to walk with us, but to live within us as well (John 14:17). God's indwelling Spirit was to make up for all the inabilities we possess in trying to accomplish righteousness. The significance from that day forward was to be "Christ in us, the hope of glory" (Col 1:27). Literally, the hope of His presence.

Certainly, we can say that the people we follow influence us, and that there can be no greater influence than that which comes from Jesus. But influence is one thing while strength and ability are quite another.

Influence inspires. It grabs the will and refocuses direction. Vision, goals, and motives come from influence. They stimulate and stir the emotions, but they don't always get the job done. Again, Paul acknowledged this when he wrote, "For I know that in me (that is in my flesh) nothing good dwells; for to will is present with me, but how to perform what is good I do not find" (Rom 7:18). Don't miss the point. Paul knew right from wrong. He understood the Law with all of its commandments. He even wanted to keep the Law. He simply did not, in and of himself, have the ability to do so. It was at this point that Paul discovered Jesus, not just in His capacity to save eternally, but also in His power to initiate changes within the soul and spirit. The result? A new creation (2 Cor 5:17), one that would live aided by God's Holy Spirit living within.

- Jesus affirmed this strength-giving principle in numerous ways:

  "And He said to me, 'My grace is sufficient for you, for My strength is made perfect in weakness'" (2 Cor 12:9).

  "For when we were still without strength, in due time Christ died for the ungodly" (Rom 5:6).

  "I am the vine, you *are* the branches. He who abides in Me, and I in him, bears much fruit; for without Me you can do nothing" (John 15:5).

- Paul spoke of His strength:

  "[F]or it is God who works in you both to will and to do for *His* good pleasure" (Phil 2:13).

- Job spoke of His strength:

"With Him *are* wisdom and strength,
He has counsel and understanding" (Job 12:13).

- The Psalmist spoke of His strength:
"I will love You, O LORD, my strength" (Psa 18:1).

"The LORD *is* my light and my salvation; Whom shall I fear? The LORD *is* the strength of my life; Of whom shall I be afraid?" (Psa 27:1).

"God *is* our refuge and strength, A very present help in trouble" (Psa 46:1).

"I will go in the strength of the Lord GOD; I will make mention of Your righteousness, of Yours only" (Psa 71:16).

"My flesh and my heart fail; *But* God *is* the strength of my heart and my portion forever" (Psa 73:26).

---

1. Sheldon, Charles. *In His Steps*. Old Tappan, NJ: Spire Books, Fleming H. Revell Company, 1971. I do not mean to criticize this book.
2. Harper, Redd. *Each Step of the Way*. Hollywood, Calif: Fiesta Music, Inc., 1952.

Chapter 13:

An Easy Yoke?

Living a good life and carrying out God's plans, desires, and commandments can appear anything but easy.

The early disciples acknowledged Jesus as the prophesied Messiah. In so doing they affirmed His lordship over them and over all creation. His will was theirs to obey. His directions were to be met with complicity. Men did not see Him as a companion with whom they could fellowship with equality, but One whose majesty was to be revered and respected. People from every walk of life recognized Him as Lord. Though He was friendly and sociable, His affable manner was still met with the reverence given only to a king.

Jesus Himself avowed His kingly role. "If you love Me, keep my commandments." But keeping commandments by way of the Law had already estranged men from God. Not that the commandments were bad, but that the flesh was weak. It was simply too hard to do right by the force of the Law.

Had Jesus stated, "These are the rules, live by them or else," not one of those men or women would have joyously continued following Him. Not because they didn't want to, but because of the element of impossibility. His followers saw Him in such a light that there was no question about who He was and the need to do His will. The issue in obeying Him was lack of ability. The power of sin was still working in them. Though they clearly heard the teaching of right and wrong, they simply could not do what was right continuously and effectively. Even while walking with Jesus, Peter's life was up and down until the Holy Spirit entered Him.

No matter how hard a person tried, a "light burden" (Mat 11:30) was still an unworkable and hopeless task, given the cancerous aspect of carnality reigning within them. Perhaps few things in life are as frustrating as being told to do something of which we have little or no capability.

It is at this point that Jesus revealed a remarkable truth that would add life to dead religion and difficult tasks. Without minimizing personal responsibility, He introduced the idea of "yoking" into the dynamics of holiness and righteousness. "Come to Me, all *you* who labor and are heavy laden, and I will give you rest. Take My yoke upon you and learn from Me, for I am gentle and lowly in heart, and you will find rest for your souls. **For My yoke *is* easy and My burden is light**" (Mat 11:28-30).

These people had been introduced to harsh legalisms and heavy burdens too hard to pull by themselves. In some cases Jesus would reduce or eliminate many of their burdens. If they would walk with Him they would find life's difficulties "light" in comparison to anything else they had ever known. In other cases His offer was that, no matter how hard the task, He would pick up the slack. He would yoke with them to get the job done.

The disciples understood well the use of oxen in regards to this word "yoke." These large beasts of burden were often fastened, side-by-side, to tackle a tiring workload. The thing that held them together was called a yoke. It was a piece of wood straddling the necks of both animals, and then fastened to the load they were to pull. It may seem a bit strange that God and man should pull together to accomplish anything, but all that anyone needs to do is to try to live Godly by themselves and any help available is welcome. In other words, we can't pull the load alone.

Why doesn't God pull without our help? God won't let us become passive by letting us watch Him get things done. We must be involved! From the beginning God destined mankind to be an intrinsic part of a relationship with Himself, a relationship so unique that currently the human mind cannot comprehend it's fullness. It is one of working together with Him to eventually reign with Him.

Most of life's frustrations are the result of trying to pull life's load alone, or of pulling with a yoke God never intended. It is a difficult yoke for anyone fighting against authority. It is a tough yoke when we want to be served, rather than to serve. It is a hard yoke when we are trying to pull the yoke of self-pity, negativism, criticism, and unforgiveness.

Perhaps the reason the early disciples became joyous men and women had much to do with this truth. John wrote, "For this is the love of God, that we keep His commandments. And His commandments are not burdensome" (1 John 5:3).

Chapter 14:

We've Got the Victory!

Overcoming sin and Satan, and living a victorious Christian life must be seen only in light of a life lived in constant communion with God. "But thanks *be* to God, who gives us the victory through our Lord Jesus Christ" (1 Cor 15:57).

Christians have a tendency to talk about victory, not so much in declaring they have it, as much as in acknowledging that victory (whatever that means) is the inherent right of a believer. In some circles the common rhetoric that follows is usually a strong emotional plea for everyone present to press forward and "get the victory." It pursues the same line of oppressive exhortation that shouts, "We've got to get our act together and do better." It articulates a condition that isn't in effect and never will be by sheer will power.

Honesty demands better of us than to try to make others and ourselves believe that everything is all right when it is not, or that by trying harder we will do better. That "all is well with my soul" before God in terms of eternity is one thing; that all is well in this life is quite another. All is not well, the battle rages everywhere. I have a couple of good days and then a bad day. I get tired, worn out, and discouraged. Am I going to make it? Absolutely! But, I'm going to make it, not because I've got the victory, but because He is the Victor and I belong to Him.

That victory, in the sense of an overcoming life, is scriptural is not debatable. The Bible is clear on the reality of living a life above sin and outside of Satan's influence. "For sin shall not have dominion over you, for you are not under law but under grace" (Rom 6:14). Scripture also assures us that in the fight against the world, the flesh, and the devil we will prevail with God's help and direction.

There is yet another very real issue involved in living a victorious life. It is the most critical of all the issues included in the subject. It is that victory, or overcoming, or whatever you want to call it, happens only in Jesus. "Who is he who overcomes the world, but he who believes that Jesus is the Son of God?" (1 John 5:5). Jesus is crucial in overcoming!

As mentioned earlier, the Scripture does not teach that we are "more than conquerors." It teaches that we are "more than conquerors *through Him*" (Rom 8:37 Italics added). This concept brings us back to the need for intimacy with Christ. The smallest movement towards fixing things on our own and by our own strength will end in disaster.

I have a book in my library that strongly suggests that an overcoming life is built on a well-disciplined lifestyle. It is a good book and few would argue against the virtues of discipline. The body and mind could use a whole lot more than most of us are willing to give. The question is not the need for discipline. The question is about the success rate of those who work to develop better lives without considering the immediate and necessary help of the Holy Spirit. William Law wrote: "The weakness of our state appears from our inability to do any thing as of ourselves. In our natural state we are entirely without any power; we are indeed active beings, but can only act by a power that is every moment lent us from God."*

If I manage to discipline my life in one area, say exercise, I generally fail or fall short in other areas such as eating. If I do manage to get most of my life under fairly good discipline, somewhere down the road much of it dissipates through neglect, laziness, or preoccupation with other things. Consistency becomes an issue. When it is all said and done, no matter how strong I may feel or think I am, I still need help. That is the point of this book. None of us by ourselves have the capability to live in a manner we know is right and correct. The flesh and the enemy of our soul put unbearable pressure on our ability to maintain a desired and needed way of life.

Only in Jesus do I find the necessary strength to live a correct lifestyle. I also find in Him the conviction and motivation to continue. Again, in and of myself, I get tired, bored, and lazy. Someone needs to remind me deep in my spirit of the necessity to go on. This is one of the advantages we have in Christ. His Spirit at work in us keeps us on the right track.

---

*. Law, William. *A Serious Call to a Devout and Holy Life.* Grand Rapids, MI; Baker Book House, Reprint 1977. p.175.

Chapter 15:

What About Discipleship?

You can train people, even animals, to do amazing things. But if their actions aren't from the heart, you've created nothing more or less than a robot.

The Greek word for "disciple" *mathetes* means "one who learns." It comes from another Greek word *manthano*, which means "to learn" or "to understand." These two words can be quite different from the definitions we put on both the words disciple and discipline today. Although the differences may seem immaterial, they are quite pronounced in their application. According to "WordWeb" from Princeton University, the word "discipline," in more modern terms means: "Training to improve strength or self-control. Train by instruction and practice; esp. to teach self-control. The trait of being well behaved. A system of rules of conduct." The suggestion is that of practicing certain actions in order to produce a desired affect.

The Greeks understood discipline to be a learning process. We understand it to be a doing process. We have a tendency to take the words disciple or discipline into a training program that emphasizes conduct and self-control. That the practice in these areas is important is evident. Training is certainly a biblical concept. The problem is that much discipleship training emphasizes personal accomplishment. Again, there is nothing wrong with that, especially in the area of developing a good physical body and mind. But when it comes to choosing and doing right, it's erroneous to think that discipline is the answer. Paul, in many of his writings, was adamant about the problem of trying to attain righteousness outside of a direct and personal relationship with Jesus. Paul never emphasized practice and hard work, the essence of modern discipline, in order to develop holiness and righteousness. Paul placed the emphasis on Jesus for righteousness. He taught the appropriation of God's Spirit as the only way to facilitate what was learned *about* righteousness. Discipline was a learning process. Once the learning was accomplished, the emphasis became Jesus as the only way to accomplish right living.

The book of Hebrews hits hard at the problem of trying to accomplish good behavior from a list of rules, followed by hard work. Its most poignant point is that guidelines for good living must be written on the heart. *"For this is the covenant that I will make with the house of Israel after those days, says the LORD: I will put My laws in their mind and write them on their hearts; and I will be their God, and they shall be My people"* (Heb 8:10).

Righteousness must come from within. And yet, with the understanding that in all of us no good thing dwells, the heart of the gospel becomes the indwelling Christ. We have no way of developing a proper lifestyle without Gods's help.

If Jesus is allowed to take up residence within the human spirit, the righteousness of the Law is fulfilled from within. The most notable aspect of this "New Covenant" administration is that a person who lives in Jesus, as Jesus lives in him, doesn't want to do wrong. Aside from problems with the flesh, righteousness is motivated from within as opposed to being dictated from without, as was common with the Law.

What About Discipleship?

Whatever kind of discipleship curriculum we may choose, we must be aware that if we are trying to discipline the self-nature of a person the effort is doomed to failure. This is no small problem. Countless ministries have failed because of this approach to ministry. The Bible doesn't teach that we get better by discipline; it teaches that our entire being needs to be changed through co-crucifixion with Jesus. Dying is the issue in changing a person (See Galatians 2:20). The Bible teaches that dying to self is the only way a person can experience life. Modern types of discipline, then, can become dangerous if they emphasize anything but the learning that leads to Christ working in us. Don't miss the point. Trying to persuade Christians to become better Christians doesn't line up with Scripture. God doesn't want to make us better people, He wants to introduce to the life that is in Jesus so that we become different people.

From another perspective it is not abundant life that we are to seek, but life that is abundant (John 10:10). Said in a different way, it is not excellence of life in terms of goods, but the amount of life in terms of relationships. "Take heed and beware of covetousness, for one's life does not consist in the abundance of the things he possesses" (Luke 12:15).

Discipline works to change the mind. It does little to change the heart. If the heart isn't changed, discipleship training only frustrates the person to whom it is directed. Try working with someone who doesn't get it no matter how hard you try to explain it. Try helping a person who says yes to everything you say and then goes out and does just the opposite. The issue is Jesus and in many cases deliverance. Often a person must be set free from bondage before he or she is ready for a true discipleship program.

Chapter 16:

Experiencing God's Presence

The words relationship and fellowship are not interchangeable. Each carries a distinct meaning that is not applicable to the other. I'm related to my sister by birth, but may not have much fellowship with her because of distance.

The same is true of Christianity. I can have a relationship with God through Jesus, but not have much fellowship with Him because of a lack of understanding of the communication system. Prayer was meant more for fellowship with God than any other thing we might conclude it to be. Prayer in its most basic state is simply getting to know God.

"He worships the ground she walks on." They worship their grandchildren." "She absolutely loves her job." No matter how you say it, it means basically the same thing—that there is much interest in, and attraction to, someone or something.

It is precisely this that is at the heart of God's desire for humanity. He wants to manifest Himself in such a way that people fall in love with Him. This is not a selfish or self-centered desire. The goal is not simply to make Him happy in the midst of His gloom. The goal is the completion of a plan so unique and wonderful that a mere glimpse into its unfolding is more breathtaking than anything found in human existence. His purpose is constant fellowship with His people. Anyone who has ever been in the presence of the Lord for any length of time knows this truth. I've asked numbers of people if they have ever felt His presence. Then I've asked if they would have liked to stay there forever and ever. The overwhelming response has been, "Yes." Can you imagine Someone touching the human spirit and triggering the desire to sit or stand in one place forever, if necessary, just to experience Him?

There comes to those who seek God the understanding that everything about who we are, as well as all of our needs, is wrapped up in God Himself. The irony and frustration is how little we perceive this in day-to-day life. That God wants me personally in His presence seems so foreign. What seems more likely is that if I work hard enough to please Him then maybe He will have mercy on me in eternity. Whatever it is about sin that turned us inward and made us cautious and even fearful of relationships is perhaps the most distinctive and destructive element of evil.

All of life and all that God has for us are found only in His presence. It is the sum total of what life is about. Our only obligation is to seek Him. Grace may take away some of the responsibility for performance (works), but it does not take away our responsibility to seek Him. "I love those who love me, /And those who **seek** me diligently will find me" (Pro 8:17-18). "And you will **seek** Me and find *Me,* when you **search** for Me with all your heart" (Jer 29:13). "**Draw near** to God and He will draw near to you" (Jas 4:8).

The story of Adam and Eve is a further confirmation of God's desire for a close relationship with humanity. Their disobedience, however, caused them to hide from God, literally from His "presence." It was this presence before they sinned that was the most significant thing in their lives. It gave them both freedom and fulfillment. While God was near they experienced none of the hellishness we experience today. That is still true today. Although the struggles of life will be with us until we die, God's presence overshadows them in ways that eliminate their destructive power. King David declared, "You will show me the path of life; /In Your **presence** *is* fullness of joy; /At Your right hand *are* pleasures forevermore" (Psa 16:11). "For You have made him most blessed forever; /You have made him exceedingly glad with Your **presence**" (Psa 21:6).

Chapter 17:

Unique Terminology

There are certain words such as "in," "through," "by," and "dwell(s) in" which refer to God's desired relationship with mankind by way of His Holy Spirit. They are words that form the essence of Christianity, and words that cannot be used by any other belief system.

In numerous places in the New Testament we are introduced to what Jesus said would happen once the Holy Spirit came to earth. Christ promised to ask the Father to send Him as soon as He returned to heaven. "And I will pray the Father, and He will give you another Helper, that He may abide with you forever—the Spirit of truth, whom the world cannot receive, because it neither sees Him nor knows Him; but you know Him, for He dwells with you and will be **in you**" (John 14:16-17).

Again, the implication is clear; God designed humanity to have a unique relationship with Himself. Just how that relationship was to be put together was, for centuries before Jesus, a mystery. When it was finally revealed, Paul the Apostle was given a primary role in its explanation. In a letter to the church at Colosse he wrote:

"I now rejoice in my sufferings for you, and fill up in my flesh what is lacking in the afflictions of Christ, for the sake of His body, which is the church, of which I became a minister according to the stewardship from God which was given to me for you, to fulfill the word of God, the mystery which has been hidden from ages and from generations, but now has been revealed to His saints. To them God willed to make known what are the riches of the glory of this mystery among the Gentiles: which is Christ in you, the hope of glory" (Col 1:24-27).

Look carefully at the words, "the mystery which has been hidden from ages and from generations." The idea of a mystery in this sense was not that of trying to figure something out, but rather recognizing that God was in the process of revealing more of His plan for mankind. The very heart of God's good news was, at that time, in the process of being revealed. And a very religious and legalistic man was chosen to disclose it. The mystery? "Christ in you, the hope of glory." Paul saw that this "glory," or "presence" of God, was the only thing that could get a person past himself or herself and into true moral rightness. Paul understood the necessity for God to do an internal work in a person if they were genuinely to become good. His constant effort to be a good man, himself, was so often met with failure that he was ready for the truth revealed in Jesus.

Now, the dots could be connected. Things that Jesus had said to His disciples were becoming easier to understand. From that day Christ's teachings would stand out against self-righteousness and false legalisms. Men would come to understand that God wanted to indwell the human spirit. That was the mystery that had been hidden. That was what Paul was now experiencing. It liberated him from religion and sent him directly into experiencing God's presence. Paul's previous efforts, backed up by his own strength and abilities, had always proven fatal to real righteousness (See Rom 7:14-26). But now he could see how much he really needed God, and how that God was willing to draw near to him to become his strength, peace, hope, and love. Christ, by His Spirit, wanted to somehow mysteriously live in him.

Listen to Jesus as He begins to reveal this truth:

"A little while longer and the world will see Me no more, but you will see Me. Because I live, you will live also. At that day you will know that **I *am* in My Father, and you in Me, and I in you**" (John 14:19-20).*

"Abide **in Me, and I in you**. As the branch cannot bear fruit of itself, unless it abides in the vine, neither can you, unless you abide **in Me**" (John 15:4).

"If you abide **in Me**, and My words abide **in you**, you will ask what you desire, and it shall be done for you" (John 15:7).

"I do not pray for these alone, but also for those who will believe in Me through their word; that they all may be one, as You, Father, *are* **in Me, and I in You**; that they also may be one **in Us**, that the world may believe that You sent Me" (John 17:20-21).

Notice how Paul carries out this theme in other passages:

"For it is God who works **in you** both to will and to do for *His* good pleasure" (Phil 2:13).

"I have told you before, and foretell as if I were present the second time, and now being absent I write to those who have sinned before, and to all the rest, that if I come again I will not spare—since you seek a proof of **Christ**

82

speaking in me, who is not weak toward you, but mighty in you" (2 Cor 13:2-3).

"But when it pleased God, who separated me from my mother's womb and called *me* through His grace, to **reveal His Son in me**, that I might preach Him among the Gentiles, I did not immediately confer with flesh and blood, nor did I go up to Jerusalem to those *who were* apostles before me; but I went to Arabia, and returned again to Damascus"(Gal 1:15-17).

"And I was unknown by face to the churches of Judea which *were* in Christ. But they were hearing only, "He who formerly persecuted us now preaches the faith which he once *tried to* destroy." And they glorified **God in me**" (Gal 1:22-24).

"[F]or He who worked effectively in Peter for the apostleship to the circumcised also **worked effectively in me** toward the Gentiles" (Gal 2:8).

"I have been crucified with Christ; it is no longer I who live, but **Christ lives in me**; and the *life* which I now live in the flesh I live by faith in the Son of God, who loved me and gave Himself for me. I do not set aside the grace of God; for if righteousness *comes* through the law, then Christ died in vain" (Gal 2:20-21).

"To this *end* I also labor, striving according to His working which **works in me** mightily"(Col 1:29).

This same element of Christ living in the human spirit is also expressed by the word "through":

"Yet in all these things we are more than conquerors **through Him** who loved us" (Rom 8:37).

"In this the love of God was manifested toward us, that God has sent His only begotten Son into the world, that we might live **through Him**" (1 John 4:9).

The principle is expressed by the word "by":

"Therefore **by Him** let us continually offer the sacrifice of praise to God, that is, the fruit of *our* lips, giving thanks to His name" (Heb 13:15).

Should there be any doubt about the meaning of these Scriptures, the following confirms that God does, indeed, desire to dwell in us by His Holy Spirit:

"For **you are the temple of the living God.** As God has said:

"I will dwell in them
And walk among them.
I will be their God,
And they shall be My people."
(2 Cor 6:16).

"Or do you not know that your body is the temple of the Holy Spirit *who is* **in you**, whom you have from God, and you are not your own?" (1 Cor 6:19).

"[T]hat He would grant you, according to the riches of His glory, to be strengthened with might through His Spirit in the inner man, that **Christ may dwell in your**

hearts through faith; that you, being rooted and grounded in love, may be able to comprehend with all the saints what *is* the width and length and depth and height—to know the love of Christ which passes knowledge; that you may be **filled with all the fullness of God**" (Eph 3:16-19).

"But you are not in the flesh but in the Spirit, if indeed the Spirit of God **dwells in you**" (Rom 8:9).

"But if the Spirit of Him who raised Jesus from the dead **dwells in you**, He who raised Christ from the dead will also give life to your mortal bodies through **His Spirit who dwells in you**" (Rom 8:11).

"Do you not know that you are the temple of God and *that* **the Spirit of God dwells in you**?" (1 Cor 3:16).

---

*. The idea here was that God would not only indwell His corporate body, but each individual as well.

Chapter 18:

It's All About Me

The "Me" generation isn't anything new. It's been around since Adam. It is so intertwined within the human frame that most of us never see it until something takes us out of ourselves and we look back and see its disdainful image.

He asked the question, "Are the promises of God for us today?" It was a simple question, one that is easy to answer. The answer of course is "Yes." Most of us who have walked with Him for any length of time can say that with confidence.

We are assured that, "[A]ll the promises of God in Him *are* Yes, and in Him Amen, to the glory of God through us" (2 Cor 1:20). "He who did not spare His own Son, but delivered Him up for us all, how shall He not with Him also freely give us all things?" (Rom 8:32). But, assuring him of God's provisions and faithfulness wasn't really the point.

It doesn't take long in life for most of us to get dug deeply into trouble. This was precisely what my friend had done. Bad decisions had cost him severely. And like anyone in trouble he was looking for a way out. He wanted to know that if he had a good relationship with God could he expect God to do something to take away the pain so present in his life. For anyone working with troubled people or trying to introduce someone to Christ, invariably the answer is, "Yes." It's "yes" because yes is the truth. God wants to give good things to His children. God wants us free from sin and its consequences.

But, the real point for this man wasn't so much God, as much as it was his own pain. If God, at that moment, had simply removed the pain, I doubt my friend would have been no different than before. This is a very difficult thing to understand, especially when we are hurting. God has much higher ideals. He wants to move us from darkness to light, from death to life. If He heals me and I continue to live in darkness, the pain simple returns.

Older Christians would, no doubt, consider my friend's motivation for serving God questionable. Serve God for any length of time and the relationship is not one of developing a Christmas catalog mentality, but one of wholehearted commitment to Him, regardless of what He gives or doesn't give. However, it may be at times as unreasonable to condemn someone for their selfishness as it is to blame a two year old for crying, especially if, in the first place, that person does not comprehend the dynamics of a relationship with God. At the same time, the issue is still that all of us are centered on ourselves, some more than others, but nevertheless all of us, and that the self-life always destroys no matter who, or how old, we are.

It is difficult to explain to someone in pain that the solution to his or her problems is not some prayer or counseling session to arbitrarily make it go away. Until the root is dealt with, the pain easily returns.

Few of us want to hear anything that does not speak directly to our difficulty. To suggest that in order to deal with the current issue we must deal with something else is not the advice we want to hear. But from the Scriptures there is no denying that in order to deal with life's pains there must be a reckoning with spiritual life in Jesus, as well as a shift in focus away from ourselves.

That I might be part of my own problem is, in itself, another problem; one that most us do not want to deal with until we are crushed very low. People made for community must have an abiding interest in others, only possible by divesting in our own self-interests.

We can see the self-interest in my friend, but may fail to see it in ourselves. From the moment we are born we are looking for what we need in order to survive. As normal as this may seem, it is precisely the thing that devastates us the most as we move through life. Self-interests that manifest themselves in selfishness are what make for a horrible world. Most of the anguish and heartache of humanity was born in the hearts of selfish people. We need to change. But like a zebra that cannot change its stripes, neither can a man change his heart. "Can the Ethiopian change his skin or the leopard its spots? *Then* may you also do good who are accustomed to do evil" (Jer 13:23). That is why God not only acknowledges this fact as far back as the Old Testament, but offers to help us even today. **"And the LORD your God will circumcise your heart** and the heart of your descendants, to love the LORD your God with all your heart and with all your soul, that you may live" (Deut 30:6). Here, again, is what this book is about—God working in people who are willing to have the work done.

Notice other Scriptures in which God is willing to change the hearts of people if they will cooperate:

"For I will set My eyes on them for good, and I will bring them back to this land; I will build them and not pull *them* down, and I will plant them and not pluck *them* up. Then I will give them a heart to know Me, that I *am* the LORD; and they shall be My people, and I will be their God, for they shall return to Me with their whole heart" (Jer 24:6-7).

"Behold, I will gather them out of all countries where I have driven them in My anger, in My fury, and in great wrath; I will bring them back to this place, and I will cause them to dwell safely. They shall be My people, and I will be their God; then I will give them one heart and one way, that they may fear Me forever, for the good of them and their children after them" (Jer 32:37-39).

"Then I will give them one heart, and I will put a new spirit within them, and take the stony heart out of their flesh, and give them a heart of flesh, that they may walk in My statutes and keep My judgments and do them; and they shall be My people, and I will be their God" (Eze 11:19-20).

There seems to be one simple thing that God is looking for in order to do an internal work in a person—that of a humble heart. This can be described by certain traits—hearts described as willing, loyal, seeking, single minded, tender, and faithful. When a heart is open to God's working, He will change it, moving it away from selfishness and into care and concern for those around him.

"'For all those *things* My hand has made,
And all those *things* exist,'
Says the LORD.
'But on this *one* will I look:
On *him who is* poor and of a **contrite spirit**,
And who **trembles at My word**'" (Isa 66:2).

For as much as God wants to work in us to establish right living (Phil 2:13), we must exercise our free will and cooperate with Him. In other words, we won't get very far in spiritual development if we don't put forth effort. The following is a helpful reminder of things necessary in order to move away from selfishness, keeping in mind that without His help our efforts are in vain (See John 15:5).

1. When you are forgotten or neglected or purposely set at naught, and you don't sting and hurt with the insult or the oversight, but your heart is happy, being counted worthy to suffer for Christ, that is dying to self.

2. When your good is evil spoken of, when your wishes are crossed, your advice disregarded, your opinions ridiculed, and you refuse to let anger rise in your heart, or even defend yourself, but take it all in patient, loving silence, that is dying to self.

3. When you are content with any food, any raiment, any climate, any society, any solitude, any interruption by the will of God, that is dying to self.

4. When you never care to refer to yourself in conversation, or record your own good works, or itch after commendation, when you truly love to be unknown, that is dying to self.

5. When you can see your brother prosper and have his needs met, and can honestly rejoice with him in spirit and feel no envy or question God, though your own needs are far greater and you are in desperate circumstances, that is dying to self.

6. When you can receive correction and reproof from someone of less stature than yourself, and can humbly submit inwardly as well as outwardly, finding no resentment or rebellion rising up in your heart, that is dying to self. (Anonymous)

But, what about my friend's problem, and ours as well? I don't want to sound trite or religious, but Job seems to be a good example of how God deals with our difficulties when we walk in His Kingdom. "And the LORD restored Job's losses when he prayed for his friends. Indeed the LORD gave Job twice as much as he had before" (Job 42:10).

Chapter 19:

Assuming Jesus

The word "religion," is generally defined as "belief in a supernatural power." But there is another definition that, if not stated, is implied—"performing in a particular way in order to create a certain lifestyle." That pretty much describes the essence of most religions. Christianity, however, was fashioned in a much different manner— different in that it was first and foremost to be the restoration of relationship with God.

Since the time of Adam men have aspired to become spiritual by way of a good life. In every culture first-rate performance and fine behavior have long been the hallmarks of what was thought to create spiritual people. Often it is the same within Christianity. But anytime behavior is put above the working of the Holy Spirit within a person, Christianity quickly descends into the same erroneous ideas and concepts of most of the religions of the world—that hard work and stringent discipline determine spiritual life.

The Christian experience may "feel" all right as long as we believe we are performing fairly well, especially while associating with other believers who think the same way. The problem is assumption. We assume that living *for* Jesus is the issue.

Let me say it again. Outside of Christianity, all world religions are wrapped up in personal performance as the only way to make a person truly spiritual. Thinking this through, they really have no other option. And why should they?

Nothing else makes sense but to try to live the best they can; at least outside of an understanding of the gospel. How often a person tries to justify himself or herself before God and others by saying, "I do the best I can and don't hurt others." This is why almost all the of Apostle Paul's ministry was focused on a new understanding concerning right living and what made for true spirituality—the integration of God's Spirit within the human spirit. This would allow for unprecedented changes that would result in a completely new life, a genuinely spiritual one. "Therefore, if anyone *is* in Christ, *he is* a new creation; old things have passed away; behold, all things have become new" (2 Cor 5:17). Don't miss the point. Paul's emphasis was that only in Christ could a person become a new creation and that this was the only way to authentic spirituality. But if that isn't taught or doesn't make sense, then the assumption is that hard work is the road to a holy life and an escape from eternal punishment.

"For we ourselves were also once foolish, disobedient, deceived, serving various lusts and pleasures, living in malice and envy, hateful and hating one another. But when the kindness and the love of God our Savior toward man appeared, not by works of righteousness which we have done, but according to His mercy He saved us, through the washing of regeneration and renewing of the Holy Spirit, whom He poured out on us abundantly through Jesus Christ our Savior, that having been justified by His grace we should become heirs according to the hope of eternal life" (Titus 3:3-7).

Chapter 20:

Legislating Holiness

The gospel message came as the good news that God, by His Son, had linked heaven and earth, making possible the fellowship that was lost in Adam. It was the process of joining a sinful people with a Holy God. But mankind has always tried to link earth with heaven by doing good deeds, by shunning certain kinds of self-described prohibitions, and by living strict lifestyles, many of which have been forced on others by unrealistic and unbiblical demands and expectations. By legislating holiness the emphasis is put on self, rather than on Jesus.

Sin has always caused humanity to perceive God as distant. If indeed He exists in the first place, it is pondered, we are galaxies away from knowing and understanding Him.

Sin is also the factor that causes the misdirection and misconduct of our lives. It tells us that we are outside of God's approval and must control ourselves better if we are to please Him.[1] In other words, to get close to God, we've got to rid ourselves of this sin that separates.

Even in light of God's mercy and forgiveness through Jesus, the sense of separation is often still with us. If we are at all God conscious we are also sin conscious. If He is holy, just, and righteous, then I must be the same in order to identify with Him. In fact, this we are clearly taught in Scripture. "[B]ut as He who called you *is* holy, you also be holy in all *your* conduct, because it is written, *"Be holy, for I am holy"* (1 Pet 1:15-16).

Realizing the distance between a Holy God and a sinful world, people have long preached the need for holiness and righteousness to close the gap, which is good. However, it is thought that these two hallmarks of a life lived pleasing to God are the performance criteria that allow Him to step out of heaven and make His presence known. Thus, the issue rests on the implementation of a lifestyle lived free from sin. Here is where the natural and spiritual minds collide. The natural mind concludes that we have the power to live godly and that force and coercion are necessary to bring sinful people into alignment with a holy God. In other words some people need to be pushed and shoved if they are to succeed. In a similar vain J.B. Phillips says:

> For, like other sentimentalists, the meek-and-mild god is in reality cruel; and those whose lives have been governed by him from early childhood have never been allowed to develop their real lives. Forced to be "loving," they have never been free to love.[2]

Likewise, forced to be good, they have never been free to be good.

If we look carefully back through history, even a few decades, most of us would be surprised at the number of believers who have fallen away. Why? A sizeable percentage of these people were constantly confronted with commandments for holy living, but left to accomplish them on their own. Nothing is more frustrating than to be told what to do, but not given the tools or the understanding of how to accomplish the task. The pressure of the resulting guilt and condemnation are more than most people can bear. As a result they sometimes wind up back in an old lifestyle or are left to struggle with the frustration of wanting to obey

God, but not knowing how, especially in light of the powerful workings of the flesh.

Innumerable people have left churches that pound hard on sin without giving hope for getting rid of it. You can hear a thousand sermons on sin and get nowhere in trying to deal with it without the direct help of the Holy Spirit. These same churches generally add unscriptural rules to their list of mandates, increasing the difficulty in living for God. Often those who leave under such duress are accused of being rebellious.

From here many who have been accosted by self-styled human conviction live under the pressurized canopy of a perverted conscience. Though God often works through the individual's conscience we are not without the possibility of deception. God's voice and the voice of conscience are not always the same.

What we learn has a marked affect on how we conduct our lives, or at least on how we think they should be conducted. My wife was taught that it was wrong to wear lipstick. Being sensitive as she is made it difficult to accept that this prohibition had no biblical foundation. I have a sense of conscience if I throw away a can that could have been recycled. For the most part, I like that. I want a conscience that is sensitive to things around me. But it can work against me if I began to feel that I have to rescue every can that is doomed for some other future. This is where ignorance produces an out of balance conscience resulting in unjustified guilt. It is also the point where legalism easily gains access into human thinking. A person with a sensitive conscience wants to make sure that no error is found in them so that there is no sense of failure, for failure means that they have yet to live well enough for God to want to close the gap between them. Therefore, it is easy to think that we must twist and squeeze ourselves into whatever standard of living is suggested that will please God.

We become discouraged in not being able to do what is right, confused over what is really right, and afraid of a God we don't understand.

The legalist works to manipulate the human conscience to produce a false sense of guilt. Whether or not he realizes this he still produces the effect. He teaches just enough truth about right living so that a person is convinced that he is right, but just enough error so that the person lives in constant fear of displeasing God. Such teaching often keeps an allegiance to the legalist through guilt, which fortifies his ego and strengthens his resolve.

Harsh and legalistic teaching and preaching makes God look much the same way. After all, it's easily concluded that this is a man of God, so he must be a spokesman for God. The pressure created by the constant exhortation to live to any standard, either Godly or manmade, compounds the gap generated by sin. It is especially the harshness of the legalist that causes many to believe they are not doing enough to please God.

If God is seen as always angry and vengeful, constantly looking for obedience that isn't possible by a person's own strength, and making strict and unreasonable demands to do better, the breach only widens. In the end, we have a tremendous amount of religion, but little of God's Spirit. The alternatives are to either give up, to justify sin, or to live a life of constant condemnation.

If we forget or don't understand the powerful inner workings of the Holy Spirit in bringing people to holiness, all preaching on living properly is in vain. "And I will pray the Father, and He will give you another Helper, that He may abide with you forever—the Spirit of truth, whom the world cannot receive, because it neither sees Him nor knows Him; but you know Him, for **He dwells with you and will be in you**" (John 14:16-17). "[F]or it is God who **works in you** both to will and to do for *His* good pleasure" (Phil 2:13).

In writing to the Philippian church Paul desired prayer from the people, and a supply of the "Spirit of Jesus Christ" from God (Phil 1:19). Here, again, Paul acknowledges the Holy Spirit in him as the only means of a life lived in righteousness, as well as one lived outside of the constant nagging of a guilty conscience.

---

1. I acknowledge that many people do not appear to consciously perceive this.
2. Phillips, J.B. *Your God Is Too Small.* New York, NY: The MacMillan Company, 1961. p.29.

Chapter 21:

A Life of Faith

Grasping the matter of faith is one of the most difficult of tasks in understanding biblical concepts. The human mind tries to figure it out while the human "will" tries to obtain it. We are seldom conscious of it either when it is present or when it is not. The fact that it is both "substance" and "evidence" is not clear to the human intellect without a revelation from God. "Now faith is the substance of things hoped for, the evidence of things not seen" (Heb 11:1).

Most Christians know they need faith in order to please God. I'm not speaking of faith in the sense of belief systems, such as the Protestant or Catholic faiths. I'm speaking of it in terms of believing God for great things. When the disciples found difficulty in carrying out the commands of Jesus in doing the miraculous, Jesus laid it on the line. "So Jesus said to them, 'Because of your unbelief; for assuredly, I say to you, if you have faith as a mustard seed, you will say to this mountain, "Move from here to there," and it will move; and nothing will be impossible for you'" (Mat 17:20).

The clear biblical directive is that faith is necessary for receiving anything from God. "But without faith *it is* impossible to please *Him,* for he who comes to God must believe that He is, and *that* He is a rewarder of those who diligently seek Him" (Heb 11:6). Understanding the concept, however, and putting it into effect is no small challenge.

A Life of Faith

Doubts and fears play games with the mind, and the spiritual dynamics behind faith get lost in a sea of confusion.

I remember as a young Christian that I spent time in prayer trying not to doubt in hopes that by doing so faith would automatically come. It didn't dawn on me at the time that the absence of doubt does not necessarily guarantee the presence of faith. No amount of mental gymnastics in *"trying"* to believe brought an ounce of faith into my life. The reason is that faith is not intrinsically resident within the human frame. No matter how far down you dig you can't find a particle of it. God alone possesses it and gives it to those who belong to Him. "[L]ooking unto Jesus, **the author and finisher of *our* faith**" (Heb 12:2). "So then faith *comes* by hearing, and hearing by the word of God" (Rom 10:17).

Judson Cornwall states this truth quite well in his book *Let Us See Jesus*.[1] "Furthermore, faith is more than positive emotions or the by-produce of religious activity. Often when I am at my lowest ebb, I haven't seen a miracle lately, my current testimony isn't worth telling, I haven't taken time to pray, I haven't fasted, and there have been no recent good works to speak of; when the Word hasn't been doing anything outstanding within me, my theology and doctrine are wavering a bit, and I have no basis for expecting faith, God mercifully opens His Word to me, imparting a believing faith that produces spiritual and natural results. I did not and could not produce it; it was totally the work and gift of God. Therefore I could never become the object of my faith, for during periods when I believe in myself the least God often flows the greatest measure of faith."

Someone may ask, 'But what about that mustard seed size faith that Jesus said could do so much?' It's still the same—all faith comes from God. Given in small quantities, it can grow to tremendous size. "For I say, through the grace given to me, to everyone who is among you, not to think *of himself* more highly than he ought to think, but to think soberly, as God has dealt to each one a measure of faith" (Rom 12:3).

Always keep in mind that this "measure" is given that it might grow. "For in it the righteousness of God is revealed from **faith to faith**; as it is written, *"The just shall live by faith"* (Rom 1:17). Notice the words "faith to faith." Faith grows when it is exercised. Don't expect to have great faith if you have neglected acting on the small faith you were first given. A man will never have great faith to do miracles until he has acted on the small faith Jesus gives to first serve others.

Again, someone may ask, "How can you have faith in something or someone you can't see, such as God?" Or, "How can you have faith in the Bible, i.e., that it is true?" Someone else will answer that faith in God isn't much different than having faith in electricity—that when you throw the switch the lights go on." Another might say, "As long as you have the key to the front door of your house you have faith that you can get in."

These illustrations as good as they may be for some, fall far short for others. Whether electricity, or a key, or something else, we were shown as a part of our teaching and training that these things work. Few of us were taught that God could be trusted or shown that the Bible is true. Even growing up in a Christian home, these basics can be more "expected" of a child rather than recognized as a necessary part of his or her training. And yet with good training a child still may question what this thing of faith is all about. The reason? Each person has to get it from God personally.

Parents and Christian teachers can encourage it and to the best of their ability show that it is real, but only Jesus can give it. And Jesus gives it to the humble person that continues to seek Him.

For those who struggle in believing anything pertaining to God, the answer for them is one of searching and pursuing, for God will manifest Himself to those whose quest is to find the truth. "And you will seek Me and find *Me,* when you search for Me with all your heart" (Jer 29:13). Oh, taste and see that the LORD *is* good; /Blessed *is* the man *who* trusts in Him! (Psa 34:8).

What about doubt? Is doubt really bad? Not necessarily, especially if it doesn't lead to unbelief. Unbelief is that dangerous place where a person quits activating the small amount of faith he has and subsequently quits his pursuit of Jesus.

All of us doubt at times. Even John the Baptist, who prepared the way for Jesus, doubted: "And when John had heard in prison about the works of Christ, he sent two of his disciples and said to Him, "Are You the Coming One, or do we look for another?" (Heb 11:2-3). Doubt generally dissipates soon after a person continues to seek truth in Jesus.

The real faith destroyers are selfishness, unforgiveness, disunity, and murmuring. You can be sure that God will not impart needed faith to those who practice ungodliness.

Perhaps, there is nothing more damaging to potential faith than the accusation that a person suffering some defeat, disease, or set back in life is doing so because of a lack of faith. Unwise and unloving Christians do great damage to others by assuming that all difficulty is brought on by faithlessness. Even if that were true, still the message of the

Scriptures is not meant to condemn, but to extend help in time of need. Those who are strong in faith got there much faster by encouragement than by condemnation.

Consider faith from another perspective. If as the Scriptures maintain there is nothing good in any of us, then personally digging up or manufacturing faith is impossible. Only Jesus possesses faith (Heb 12:2), and only He can give it (Rom 10:17). People who are having difficulty in any area of life need to be encouraged to get faith from Jesus without harassment.

From still another perspective, Oswald Chambers observed, "Faith is rooted in the knowledge of a Person, and one of the biggest traps we fall into is the belief that if we have faith, God will surely lead us to success in the world."[2]

---

1. Cornwall, Judson. *Let Us See Jesus*. South Plainfield, New Jersey: Bridge Publishing, Inc., 1981. pp 48-49.
2. Chambers, Oswald. *My Utmost For His Highest*. Electronic Edition STEP Files Copyright © 1998, Parsons Technology, Inc., all rights reserved. March 19 devotion.

Chapter 22:

Personal Guidance

Most of the emphasis of this book has been on the personal work of the Holy Spirit within us. Much of His work is to bring about holiness and righteousness in the life of a believer. Our own endeavors without His help easily end in failure. It is precisely for this reason that we so desperately need Him, especially in regards to conquering both the flesh and the devil. Of all that He does for us, there is still one work of His that we must not overlook—that of guidance. Fulfillment in life is directly related to knowing God's will.

God's guidance is not something we cry out for in the midst of our pain with the attitude that if He is really God He has to answer, especially if we have no established relationship with Him through Jesus. This is not to say that He is aloof or insensitive. Certainly, God reaches to people when they call on Him, no matter who or where they are at in life. It is to say that to get Him to step into our lives we can't just call on Him in trouble and then when the difficulty is past go on our own way once again. That approach presses the limits on any relationship.

God is looking for deep-seated and permanent relationships. The following Scriptures may be sobering, but they are important in our understanding of how He works. They are meant to put us on a footing where God can begin to do something powerful in our lives on a continual basis.

Notice, first, that God wants our allegiance—fully, completely, and without reservation. As in a marriage no half measure will work. "So then, because you are lukewarm, and neither cold nor hot, I will vomit you out of My mouth" (Rev 3:16).

Second, God declares that we cannot serve more than one master at a time. In this case He makes it plain that it is not only people who become our masters, but things such as money as well. "No one can serve two masters; for either he will hate the one and love the other, or else he will be loyal to the one and despise the other. You cannot serve God and mammon" (Mat 6:24).

Third, God wants us involved in His plan for this planet, and we are either with Him or against Him in carrying out His goals. "He who is not with Me is against Me, and he who does not gather with Me scatters abroad" (Mat 12:30).

And fourth, God is looking for Kingdom minded people, those who want to be a part of everything He is about. "But seek first the kingdom of God and His righteousness, and all these things shall be added to you" (Mat 6:33).

Don't miss the point! God is not selfish in wanting our attention both completely and wholeheartedly. The spiritual battles currently waged here and in the heavenlies disallow any aspect of selfishness on the part of those who join Him. Right now the war is too serious for anyone to live for himself or herself.

Making these commitments opens us to the personal guidance of the Holy Spirit. Without robbing us of free will, God now gives directions for fulfilling His purpose in us. But hearing God is of major importance when, even as Christians, we are capable of falling into deception. We are warned in Scripture not to be deceived (See Luke 21:8 and Gal 6:7). Human desire and demon spirits often play havoc in our quest for determining God's will. And not a few have affirmed their belief in God's direction by simply saying, "God told me!" when, in fact, it was not His voice. But how can we be reasonably sure it is God speaking? Here are five foundational thoughts to keep in mind.

1. Is the directive in line with Scripture? To argue with the Scriptures is pointless if we really want what God wants. You can't say it's God's will to get a divorce simply because you have fallen out of love with your spouse. The Scriptures are clear on this. You can't lie, cheat, and steal because everyone else is doing it, or it seems good in the case of situational ethics. God does not affirm what the Scriptures deny.

2. Is the Holy Spirit bringing conviction to my spirit? He has been called "The Hound of Heaven," meaning that the Holy Spirit will bring either caution or approval to the human spirit when we are a part of God's Kingdom. His warnings are sensed deep in the spirit and become a safeguard against error. But we can neglect His warnings to the point we are no longer able to hear His voice. "[S]peaking lies in hypocrisy, having their own conscience seared with a hot iron" (1 Tim 4:2). In order for conviction to work there must be a standard of conduct. That standard is the Scriptures. When the Word and the Spirit agree it is simply the Holy Spirit bringing our knowledge of God's Word to bear on our actions.

3. Are the doors opening for fulfilling His will? God makes plain His call or directive as doors are opened. We may not see them entirely at first, but can be assured that our first steps will be met with a way to accomplish His will. "He

[Abraham] went out, not knowing where he was going" (Hebrews 11:8).
4. Does it agree with wise counsel? Only an arrogant and unwise person claims to get direction solely from God and doesn't need help from others. Who, in really wanting God's will, seeks to get it from mankind anyhow. Only God knows what He wants for each of His children. At the same time the Holy Spirit often works through other believer's, not to give God's will, but to confirm it. In this way we are better able to avoid deception.
5. Even if we are somewhat reluctant to do His will, especially out of fear, by continuing to seek Him He creates a desire to do it. "[F]or it is God who works in you both to will and to do for *His* good pleasure" (Phil 2:13).

"A wise *man* will hear and increase learning, /And a man of understanding will attain wise counsel" (Pro 1:5).

"Plans are established by counsel; /By wise counsel wage war" (Pro 20:18).

"For by wise counsel you will wage your own war, /And in a multitude of counselors *there is* safety" (Pro 24:6).

Chapter 23:

The Problem of Pride

I have little doubt that there is anything in life more damaging than pride. It may well be that when we reach the end of this life and realize more fully what is was all about, that we will see that pride was the most sinister of all things we faced.

From the very beginning pride was the element that caused all the devastating things we see in our world today. It was the first ingredient in the mixture that originally poisoned the human race. It is obvious from Adam's response to God's inquiry as to why he and his wife had disobeyed His clear and unmistakable directives for their lives that Adam had become arrogant. In Genesis 3:12, after God had asked him if he had disobeyed, Adam dodges the question by responding, "It's not my fault." In essence, He challenges God by saying, "Listen, it's all your fault for giving me this woman, and it's her fault because of what she did in listening to the serpent." What might history have been like if Adam had simply owned up to his disobedience? Would the human race have suffered less if Adam had said, "God, you're right, I disobeyed you and I'm sorry. What can I do to make up for the wrong I have done?" We may never know if history would have been different, but although I would like to believe that it would have been, I seriously doubt it. There would still have been the need for a Savior, the need for deliverance, and all of the rest of the redemption story, as we understand it today.

Adam's sin has got to be understood as more than just a little blip on his personal radar screen. It wasn't a matter of just "admit it and say you are sorry." This was a monumental break in a relationship. It was the imparting of an attitude as contrary as it could possibly be to God's design for him personally.

Pride is the substance that destroys relationships, even that of a relationship with God. Perhaps we could say that selfishness is pride's most prominent display. It desires the focus and attention of people around it, most often to the point of minimizing their worth. It is the element that demands control over everything within its grasp. Given full reign it will eventually, similar to its work in Lucifer, cause a person to claim to be "like God" in its preeminence.

For as lethal as pride is, it is quite difficult to see or perceive, especially in ourselves. We have lived around it so long it seems like a normal part of life. A pig doesn't smell bad to itself.

Only when we observe pride in its extreme are we even conscious that it exists. Observing a person who is determined to get his or her way at any cost should alert us to its presence. Like a deadly virus, pride lurks unseen until its affects have ruined a life. And then most of the time we still are not aware of what caused the damage.

Dismiss pride as unimportant to what you are facing and your chances of seeing a solution are virtually nil. Try to conqueror it with the best of regret, remorse, and sorrow that you can muster up and you still won't win. Say that you will look into it more closely when you get the time and the time will never come. It is through a distorted understanding of the devastating power of pride that we fall prey to its toxic presence.

Another sad aspect of its reality is that it is found in every human being alive. No one escapes it. The fact that we seldom detect it in our own lives only serves to verify its subtlety. To say that we have no pride is pride itself. To try to dispose of it through piety, penitence, or a somber attitude is to paint a religious coating over it.

Pride is also the first thing that God must deal with if we are to have a relationship with Him. But you can hear its ugly rhetoric when it is exposed to truth:

God says there is salvation in no other than Jesus. Pride says I want numerous ways to get to God.

God says only the blood of Jesus cleanses from sin. Pride says I have no sin from which to be cleansed.

God says you can't serve God and money. Pride says I can't live without abundance.

God says come out and away from the influences of the world. Pride says there is nothing out there that will hurt me.

For whatever God says, pride brings a contradiction.

Pride goes on to ruin believers, as well, when it subtlety suggests that a person in Christ is free from its influence. The resting place of many unsuspecting Christians is the graveyard of "spiritual" pride. But the disposition of pride within us makes it impossible for us to deal with it. So powerful is its influence, its root and character, that no human being can cut it away from himself. Only Jesus can draw it out of our very nature, and that only by a humility that is willing for the work to be done. Andrew Murray explains:

> Man's chief care, his highest virtue, and his only happiness, now and through eternity, is to present himself as an empty vessel in which God can dwell and manifest His power and goodness.

The life God bestows is imparted not once and for all, but each moment continuously, by the unceasing operation of His mighty power. Humility, the place of entire dependence on God, is, from the very nature of things, the first duty and the highest virtue of man. It is the root of every virtue.

And so pride, or the loss of this humility, is the root of every sin and evil.[1]

Paul Billheimer writes:

Very few can take honors, either from the world or from God, without becoming conceited. What servant of the Lord does not know the subtle temptation to spiritual pride that follows even mediocre success? How often one relates an answer to prayer in such a way as to reflect credit upon oneself—and then ends up blandly saying "To God be the glory." The ego is so swollen by the fall that it is an easy prey to Satan and his demons....Who knows how much God would do for His servants if He dared. If one does not boast openly following an anointed fluency of speech, a specific answer to prayer, a miracle of faith or some other manifestation of spiritual gifts, or even graces, he is tempted to gloat secretly because of the recognition. Except for special grace on such occasions, one falls easily into Satan's trap. Because most men are so vulnerable to any small stimulus of pride, God although He loves to do so, dares not honor many before the world by special displays of His miracle working power in answer to prayer.

For until God has wrought a work of true humility and brokenness in His servants, He cannot answer some of their prayers without undue risk of producing the pride that goes before a fall. If God could trust the petitioner to keep lowly, who knows how many more answers to prayer He would readily give.[2]

In the previous chapters of this book I've tried to draw attention to Scriptures that lead to a closer walk with Jesus—passages that emphasis God working in us. But, lamentably, there are dangers. The knowledge He gives can easily lead to pride if not carefully guarded. "Knowledge puffs up, but love edifies" (1 Cor 8:1). But it is not just knowledge. A walk with God can also lead to making comparisons and value judgments about others. When we see some people more carnal and distant from God than ourselves, we easily believe that we are better or more advanced. C.S. Lewis believed that the pride found in making comparisons was basically competitive:

Now what you want to get clear is that Pride is essentially competitive—is competitive by its very nature—while the other vices are competitive only, so to speak, by accident. Pride gets no pleasure out of having something, only out of having more of it than the next man. We say that people are proud of being rich, or clever, or good-looking, but they are not. They are proud of being richer, or cleverer, or better looking than others. If everyone else became equally rich, or clever, or good-looking there would be nothing to be proud about. It is the comparison that makes you proud: the pleasure of being above the rest. Once the element of competition has gone, pride has gone.[3]

If pride is the root of all of our problems, then humility is the solution. But we will get nowhere with humility until we understand its importance and power. For most of us our initial response is one of distaste. Humility suggests pushing ourselves down. Some feel that to be truly humble a person must lose his or her personality, uniqueness, and identity. It also suggests that a person must become a virtual doormat to everyone else in life. But none of these things are true. Humility is more an ongoing set of actions than it is a condition. It has more to do with what we do than how we feel about God, others, and ourselves. Humility before God has no meaning if it is not worked out in relationships with people.

How foreign it may be to some to think that great leaders could be humble men and women. It simply does not seem to satisfy the definition of greatness. "(Now the man Moses *was* very humble, more than all men who *were* on the face of the earth.)" (Num 12:3). This great leader was a humble man only because of his actions in response to God's call on his life.

The Apostle Paul warned against immaturity in leadership, noting that it had great potential in leading one into being "puffed up with pride," the outcome of which was to "fall into the same condemnation as the devil." (See 1 Tim 3:6). "A man's pride will bring him low, but the humble in spirit will retain honor" (Pro 29:23).

Pride is no small vessel on the sea of life. It is a pirate ship searching diligently to find its prey, and once you are in range it will bear down on you with guns blazing. But the major question has to do with how it is attached to what I am personally facing at the moment. How could something I am vaguely aware of, and something that usually only applies to the person who flaunts his existence, be attached to me?

It is at this point that the subject needs to be qualified before we continue. You may be saying, "My problem is my husband and our relationship. How does that relate to pride?" And while thinking about this particular predicament, the question is where is this so-called pride in me that keeps my problems alive? Adam's disgrace has affected all of us have the disease. Pride is like a stubborn infection that we came in contact with when we were born. And when you discover it, it is always the ME thing—my pain, my hurt, my opinions, my rights, and my wants and desires.

More than a few people will affirm that it wasn't until they humbled themselves before God that they began to see resolve in their circumstance. The simple act of bringing God into the equation was the antiseptic that brought healing to a troubled marriage, or whatever other difficulty they were facing. Humility destroys pride. "Humble yourselves in the sight of the Lord, and he will lift you up" (Jas 4:10).

One of the first traits of humility is the willingness to listen, learn, and obey. We humble ourselves when we seek to build relationships. We humble ourselves when we are willing to admit our mistakes. We humble ourselves when we stop to consider the feelings of another. And most important, we humble ourselves when we ask God to make us into new people—to take away our sin and rebellion against Him and others.

Perhaps nothing answers the questions surrounding our need for humility more than does the life of Jesus. If Jesus needed to humble Himself, how much more for you and me: "And being found in appearance as a man, **He humbled Himself** and became obedient to *the point of* death, even the death of the cross" (Phil 2:8). "*Let* nothing *be done* through selfish ambition or conceit, but in lowliness of mind let each esteem others better than himself. Let each of you look out not only for his own interests, but also for the interests of others. Let this mind be in you which was also in Christ Jesus, who, being in the form of God, did not consider it robbery to be equal with God, but made Himself of no reputation, taking the form of a bondservant, *and* coming in the likeness of men. And being found in appearance as a man, **He humbled Himself** and became obedient to *the point of* death, even the death of the cross" (Phil 2:3-8).[4]

---

1. Murray, Andrew. *Humility*. Springdale, PA; Whitaker House, 1982. p.10.
2. Billheimer, Paul. *Destined for the Throne*. Fort Washington, PA; Christian Literature Crusade, 1975. pp.98-99.
3. Lewis, C.S. *Mere Christianity*. New York; MacMillan Publishing Co., Inc. , 1943, 1945, 1952. pp.109-110.
4. Quote from a friend of mine: "I have sometimes likened our spiritual journey to traveling down a very long hallway with mirrors on both sides. We tend, on the journey, to continuously be looking in one mirror or the other; either smugly to the one on our right which shows how good we look, or disgustedly to the one on our left which shows how badly we are doing, and both are driven by pride. The key is the focus on the self.

Meanwhile, at the far end of the hallway stands Jesus. The trick is to fix our eyes on him and never bother looking in the mirrors at all. It seems to me that the devil's chief effort with us, at least with Christians, is to distract us from looking unto Jesus, and he can most easily do that by getting us to focus on both our successes and our failures. Either one is equally effective in distracting us from the Lord." Darrel Faxon

Chapter 24:

Doing the Father's Will

One of the most important aspects of Christ's mission to earth was His determination to do the Father's will without the slightest concern for His own.

"I am the vine, you *are* the branches. He who abides in Me, and I in him, bears much fruit; for without Me you can do nothing" (John 15:5). Just as Jesus proclaimed that we could do nothing without Him, He taught that He maintained a similar relationship with the Father. "Then Jesus answered and said to them, 'Most assuredly, I say to you, the Son can do nothing of Himself, but what He sees the Father do; for whatever He does, the Son also does in like manner'" (John 5:19).

When this understanding permeates ever part of our existence and especially our ministries, bringing us to call on God for help in everything, we move into the very ways in which Jesus did things, and that was to allow the Father to work in Him. "Do you not believe that I am in the Father, and the Father in Me? The words that I speak to you I do not speak on My own *authority;* but the Father who dwells in Me does the works" (John 14:10). Now it is Christ who works in us. "[F]or it is God who works in you both to will and to do for *His* good pleasure" (Phil 2:13).

Because Jesus is God (Col 1:16; 1 Tim 3:16), we may assume that He operated here on earth in regards to the way he saw things—that is, He looked on situations and circumstances determining what needed to be done, and then set about making things happen. Not so!

116

So complete was the Son's submission to the Father that everything Jesus did was in direct obedience to Him. Nothing of what Christ personally possessed, as the Second Person of the Godhead, was ever manifested in His ministry here on earth. Every bit of wisdom, every miracle, every prophecy, and every desire, all came from the Father. Jesus' only intent was to glorify the Father. "And whatever you ask in My name, that I will do, that the Father may be glorified in the Son" (John 14:13). "Now My soul is troubled, and what shall I say? 'Father, save Me from this hour'? But for this purpose I came to this hour. Father, glorify Your name" (John 12:27-28). To Him it was all about the Father and the Father's will. Christ's life was a life of perfect submission and dependency. "Jesus answered them and said, 'My doctrine is not Mine, but His who sent Me'" (John 7:16). "Then Jesus cried out, as He taught in the temple, saying, 'You both know Me, and you know where I am from; and **I have not come of Myself, but He who sent Me is true**, whom you do not know'" (John 7:28).

If, indeed, we are to do the works of Jesus, we must operate with dependence on Him just as He operated with dependence upon the Father. "Most assuredly, I say to you, he who believes in Me, the works that I do he will do also; and greater *works* than these he will do, because I go to My Father" (John 14:12). "Jesus said to them, 'If God were your Father, you would love Me, for I proceeded forth and came from God; **nor have I come of Myself, but He sent Me**'" (John 8:42).

But, it is not just our need for dependence upon Jesus; it is also a complete determination to do His will over ours. Alignment with God's will as determined by the Scriptures is an absolute. There is no way to work for Him if I'm not willing to do what He wants done. This is precisely the manner in which Jesus worked in regards to the Father's will. "He who does not love Me does not keep My words; and the word which you hear is not Mine but the Father's who sent Me" (John 14:24).

It is in Gethsemane that Christ's determination to do the Father's will is put to its final test. "He went a little farther and fell on His face, and prayed, saying, 'O My Father, if it is possible, let this cup pass from Me; nevertheless, not as I will, but as You *will*'" (John 26:39).

What would have happened if Jesus had said, "No" to the Father? If it could have happened, a matter of speculation and I suppose intense theological debate, it is obvious that salvation would not have been possible, and we would have been assigned to an eternity without God. That is pretty severe and, again, speculative. What is not speculation are the results of decisions in which we maintain our will over God's will. Human suffering and sorrow are the consequences of disallowing His will in human affairs.

Independence is far more of a problem than most of us would like to think. I don't know how many times I've tried to put something together without consulting the manual—without following the directions. It can be the same with the things of the Lord. How often we learn something and then set about making it known to everyone around us. Ministry is like that. I learn something new and immediately go about teaching it, seldom thinking that God might have something different for my audience. "Then Jesus said to them, 'When you lift up the Son of Man, then you will know that I am *He,* and *that* **I do nothing of Myself**; but as My Father taught Me, I speak these things'" (John 8:28).

118

Hence, submission to the Father's will, in total rejection of His own, was the only way the work of the Father was ever to be accomplished. And the same thing is true of us. It is only as we are submitted to God's will, in rejection of our own, that God's work is going to be accomplished. This fact is a reality in respect to both God's work *in* us (the change into his character) and his work *through* us (whatever ministry it is that he has given us). And given the fact that the work of ministry (Ephesians 4:12-13) is for the purpose of bringing all the saints to the measure of the stature of the fullness of Christ, that submission of the will is critical at both levels.

Chapter 25:

"I Will Awake in Your Likeness."

God's eternal plan is to provide a bride for His Son. To do so He is preparing her right now for the wedding day.

For God to have His desired relationship with humanity, we would have to have some kind of unique similarity *to* Him in order to identify *with* Him. "Then God said, 'Let Us make man in /Our **image**, according to /Our **likeness**'" (Gen 1:26). Much, if not most, of God's workings in us is to bring us back into what He originally created us to be. Thus, He focuses on shaping our character so that we might commune with Him on common ground. God's ultimate purpose is to have a people with whom He can rule and reign over the universe. "If we endure, /We shall also reign with *Him*" (2 Tim 2:12).

The Psalmist, with his deep yearning to know God, knew he needed to be different if his desire was to be realized. "As for me, I will see Your face in righteousness; **I shall be satisfied when I awake in Your likeness**" (Psa 17:15). "Likeness," in this case, has to do with forming the character of Jesus in us. "For whom He foreknew, He also predestined *to be* **conformed to the image of His Son**" (Rom 8:29). We already have, we might say, God's DNA in us, at least in a spiritual sense. It is His character we lack, and that which must be restored.

All of God's work in us here on earth is to bring us to Himself. From there He wants to let His character and personality rub off on us. Most of the changes needed for a

120

relationship with Him occur as we become willing to allow for them to take place in us. This is much of what prayer is about—experiencing His presence, and the change it brings. "Beloved, now we are children of God; **and it has not yet been revealed what we shall be, but we know that when He is revealed, we shall be like Him**, for we shall see Him as He is. And everyone who has this hope in Him purifies himself, just as He is pure" (1 John 3:2-3). "For our citizenship is in heaven, from which we also eagerly wait for the Savior, the Lord Jesus Christ, **who will transform our lowly body that it may be conformed to His glorious body**, according to the working by which He is able even to subdue all things to Himself" (Phil 3:20-21). Don't miss the point. The Father is working in His people, developing in them character fit for His presence. The only measure of that character is Jesus.

Change is the issue. "Therefore, if anyone *is* in Christ, *he is* **a new creation**; old things have passed away; behold, all things have become new" (2 Cor 5:17). "For in Christ Jesus neither circumcision nor uncircumcision avails anything, but **a new creation**" (Gal 6:15). But the Scriptures are explicit; only God can make the needed changes. I must cooperate for He will not force me to do so. "Then he said to me, 'Do not fear, Daniel, for from the first day that you set your heart to understand, and to **humble yourself** before your God, your words were heard; and I have come because of your words'" (Dan 10:12).

Christians have the tendency to try to be the best possible people they can be, using all of their own personal abilities to be good. This often happens in view of the sin they desperately want to get rid of, or because of a pressing need for which they want His help. But the issue is not trying to be a better person for whatever reason—the issue is becoming new, literally being transformed. "And do not be conformed to this world, but **be transformed** by the renewing of your mind, that you may prove what *is* that good and acceptable and perfect will of God" (Rom 12:2). "But we all, with unveiled face, beholding as in a mirror the glory of the Lord, are being transformed into the same image from glory to glory, just as by the Spirit of the Lord" (2 Cor 3:18).

God's Word, along with His presence and grace, work both to bring us to Jesus to be molded into His image and likeness. "[F]or it is **God who works in you** both to will and to do for *His* good pleasure" (Phil 2:13). [B]eing confident of this very thing, that **He who has begun a good work in you will complete *it*** until the day of Jesus Christ" (Phil 1:7).

Don't Miss The Point! All of life is meant for the purpose of becoming like Jesus by way of His indwelling Holy Spirit.